America's
MARK TWAIN

by MAY McNEER

with illustrations by LYND WARD

Houghton Mifflin Company Boston

The Comet

IN THE YEAR 1835 people came from their houses to bend back their heads and search the dark night sky for a glimpse of a flaming visitor leaving a brilliant trail across the heavens. This was a comet called Halley's, in honor of an English astronomer who had predicted its seventy-sixth-year orbit.

"Look! Look! The comet." Those who knew what it was pointed and exclaimed and wondered how Edmund Halley could have known that it would return when predicted? Those who did not know turned away frightened, and thought that it must be a sign that the end of the world was at hand. On the edge of the frontier, where a great river divided the continent of America, where the United States ended and the prairies and wild plains began, the tiny crossroads village of Florida, Missouri, looked upward too.

Jane Clemens, standing beside her husband at the window, drew her gray wool shawl closer about chilly shoulders and bent forward to see the fiery visitor in the sky. She could hear the excited voices of her sister and her sister's husband, John Quarles, and their children as they joined the neighbors in the frozen mud of the road.

Two weeks later, on November 30, while the shining comet still swept across the darkness, a son was born to Jane and John Marshall Clemens. They named him Samuel Langhorne Clemens, and called him "Little Sam." This was a small and sickly baby, and there was some doubt that he would live to grow up. He joined a family poor in purse and rich in pride. Brother Orion was an awkward ten-year-old; sister Pamela, gentle and helpful, looked after small Margaret and Benjamin. Judge Clemens was a lawyer and a Justice of the Peace, stern and unsmiling — a man of principle, but one with a dreamy impractical nature. He had married red-haired, fun-loving Jane Lampton in Tennessee, and had given her a life that was crowded with failure. The family had lived in one country village after another, often in poverty, yet the judge — so called because he was a Justice of the Peace — always held before their dazzled eyes a vision of a vast fortune in the distant future.

Judge Clemens owned some acreage in wild land in Tennessee and believed that one day it would be of immense value. While waiting for land values to rise, he kept store when he could not practice law. Yet his chief interest was always aroused by some impractical scheme for making money, as well as by various inventions of his own — such as a machine that would produce perpetual motion.

When Judge Clemens failed to earn a living as a lawyer in Florida, he moved his family to a larger town called Hannibal,

on the western banks of the Mississippi River. Here he opened a grocery store, and built a small house of white-painted boards, like the other houses in Hannibal.

"Little Sam" was the only child in the family who was not born strong and sturdy, yet he survived when both Margaret and Benjamin died of childhood diseases. Under a mop of sandy-red curls Little Sam's gray eyes looked innocent enough — until a gleam of mischief would appear. He was very much like his mother and he enraged her one minute and made her laugh the next. His funny way of speaking Jane called "Sammy's slow talk," but it was an echo of her own. Before he was old enough to go to school Sammy was already giving her more trouble than her other children ever did. His innocent face hid an imagination and a sense of mischief that caused his harassed mother to shake her head and say, "Sammy is a well of truth, but you can't bring it up in one bucket."

5

Nowhere in the whole exciting country could a boy find a better place to live in than Hannibal, Missouri. Between Holliday's Hill and the bluffs called Lovers' Leap, the village of white frame houses and log cabins drowsed in the sun. Westward the prairie edges were already being invaded by farmers, and fields of wheat and corn fringed the wilderness. Eastward, Hannibal saw the sun rise over the broad and muddy waters of the Mississippi, with a distant line of Illinois forest beyond, and islands standing green along both shores. Bear Creek made swimming holes for boys who learned to move like fish in its stream — or drowned trying. Sam Clemens always said that he was almost drowned nine times before he grew up, but his mother made the tart remark that she didn't worry. A boy born to be hanged was safe in the water.

To the Indians, the Mississippi had been the "Father of Waters." To the people of Hannibal it was a broad highway, taking their products to market, providing means of travel, bringing in goods and visitors. To everybody, but especially to the boys, it was excitement — a gaudy, gleeful, glittering excitement.

When the cry rose, "Steamboat a-com–in!" suddenly the sleepy town came alive. The Negro drayman was usually the first to raise the shout, boys right behind him, pelting down the hill. There she came, whistle blowing, steaming up to the dock, her gilded stacks gleaming! Passengers crowded the railing while the great, awe-inspiring pilot brought her into the landing. He stood on deck, pipe in mouth, looking loftily down on the boys as passengers climbed the gangplank. Every boy in Hannibal wanted to become a pilot on a river steamboat. Every boy dreamed proud dreams of piloting the glittering floating palaces; and when a boy was not imagining himself a pilot, then he pretended to be the steamboat itself — backing and turning, making steaming and whistling noises, up and down the streets of Hannibal.

Second only to the river, the busy, active Quarles farm was the most interesting spot to Sammy. Every summer the Clemens family went there to visit Jane's sister and brother-in-law. Hearty John Quarles, with his long hair and big laugh, was the pattern that all uncles should have been made by. Sammy played with his cousins and the slave children. Some nights he followed the coon hunters and returned at dawn with the tired Quarles men, slaves, and packs of dogs to eat a huge breakfast on the porch connecting the two big log cabins that made the farmhouse. Other nights Sammy lingered by the wide fireplace listening to the moaning sound of his aunt's spinning wheel, or he joined the many children gathered in the kitchen. Negroes sat there telling fearsome stories of old Raw Head and Bloody Bones — or the tale of "The Golden Arm." That one sent chills racing down Sammy's spine, no matter how many times he heard it, and he went off to bed shivering with fright. But it was his favorite, just the same.

One morning of the summer before Sammy was four, Jane gathered her children into the wagon to go to the farm. Since Sammy was still asleep, she left him and asked his father to bring him later when he came on horseback. When Sammy awakened the house was dim and there wasn't a sound. The doors and windows were all locked. As the day wore on Sammy cried a little, went to play with cornmeal leaking from a sack in the kitchen, and then grew terrified, for he felt sure his family had deserted him. Meantime his father, delayed until evening, had forgotten that he was to pick up Sammy.

When the judge arrived at the farm, thirty miles away, Jane

demanded, eyes flashing, "Where's Sammy?"

Sam's father looked surprised. "Why, I do believe that I forgot the boy," he said.

Before his wife could unloose her wrath, one of the younger uncles leaped onto his horse and was off to the rescue. Sam never forgot that day in the desolate abandoned house.

Sammy was sent to school at the age of four and a half. His teachers were two dignified ladies, Mrs. Horr and her spinster daughter, who taught the younger children of Hannibal in a small log cabin. On his second day Sammy disobeyed his teacher. Mrs. Horr sternly told him to go out and pick a switch for his own punishment. Sammy found several bushes bearing switches, but couldn't bring himself to break one off. Across the way a cooper's shop was puncturing the pleasant spring day with the noise of planing that sent long shavings into the dusty street. Sammy returned to Mrs. Horr with a curled shaving in hand, and solemnly presented it for a switch. The outraged teacher not only sent out for one that would sting Sammy's unfortunate legs but also reported his impudence to his mother.

As "Little Sam" became "Sammy" and "Sammy" grew old
enough to be called "Sam," the devilish twinkle in his innocent
face came more frequently. His schooldays, though filled with
troubles, were not without fun. Sam scarcely ever came to school
without bringing a pinch bug in a box, to set loose in a quiet
moment, or persuading John Briggs to put a verse on the
blackboard — a verse about "Cross Mr. Cross" — or doing some
other devilment. But it was the thought of Saturday that
dominated Sam's life. Sometimes he played hooky because he
couldn't wait for the end of the week.

Sam had a brother, Henry, who was two years younger than
he. Henry was handsome and good, whereas Sam was only
handsome — when dressed for Sunday School. Sam was strong
and was no longer expected to die young, especially since it was
generally believed that only the good die young. Henry, on the
other hand, was a great help to his mother. He took delight in
helping her keep tabs on Sam. When Jane sent Sam off to Mr.
Cross's school of a morning she sewed his shirt at the collar so
that she could tell whether he had played hooky to go swim-

ming with Tom Blankenship, son of the town drunkard. And when she nodded in satisfaction at suppertime, seeing that it was still sewed, who but Henry would sing out, "Ma, didn't you sew Sam's shirt with white thread? It's fastened with black now."

For that favor Sam threw clods of mud at Henry, and his opinion of Mother's good boy didn't rise into respect until Henry retaliated by pelting him back with stones.

Mrs. Clemens' punishments came in the form of work. On a Saturday morning just made for fishing in a "borrowed" rowboat and for the company of tattered Tom Blankenship, Sam had to whitewash the fence. To add insult to injury Sam's best friends — John Briggs, Will and Sam Bowen, and others — passed by, fishing rods trailing over shoulders. One morning, gazing mournfully down at a large pail of whitewash, Sam had a flash of genius. He would make his friends believe that whitewashing a fence was a privilege. When they began to ask permission, he was so reluctant to give up the brush, that they gave him their valuables in order to be allowed to whitewash — old doorknobs, apple cores, frogs, and a box of worms, among other things.

When Jane Clemens came out to check on his progress, she found Sam gone, and, stretching out before her eyes a long, freshly whitewashed fence. She shook her head. "How that boy could paint so fast beats me. It just beats me to here and gone!"

Although Sam grew to be as tough as a ranging colt, his mother seemed quite unaware that his health had improved. She was still in the habit of forcing all sorts of medicine into him, from sulphur and molasses to a black noxious fluid simply called "Pain-killer." One day Sam gave a dose of Pain-killer to the favorite of all his mother's nineteen cats. When she reproached him for causing the poor animal to climb the walls in a frenzy, Sam said, in his funny, slow way, that he was only doing Peter good. If that stuff was good for a boy why wasn't it good for a cat?

Sam Clemens' inventiveness brought him many friends. The boys of Hannibal were constantly forming themselves into bands of various kinds, and Sam was the leader of every band. He was the Avenger of the Spanish Main, the chief Knight of the Round Table, Robin himself in the Band of Merry Men, and Blackbeard the Pirate. These rousing gangs operated in the woods on Holliday's Hill, sometimes with the added pleasure of Tom Blankenship's company.

More often, though, Tom went fishing, and condescended, as was the way of a great man, to take along Sam and John and Will. Tom knew the best holes where the biggest catfish could be caught. He knew the place to hunt for turtle eggs on the islands, and he taught the other boys to smoke corncob pipes and swear. Tom Blankenship was the envy of Sam and all of his friends. He slept in a hogshead barrel, and was nothing but a "ruin of rags," as Sam said, but nobody told him what to do, or how to do it. He didn't have to go to school to Mr. Cross, or to the Presbyterian Sunday School in a clean shirt, after a painful scrubbing behind the ears.

Tom's hogshead was in a broken-down barn just behind Sam's house. On many an evening when his shrill catcall came to Sam's ears, Sam would wait until Henry was asleep and slide down the porch roof to go off with Tom. They would visit the cemetery, carrying a dead cat to cure warts, or dig for a treasure supposedly buried near the village by the hideous Murrel gang of robbers some years before.

Though Sam felt that wielding a paintbrush on a fence was more hard work than he should be asked to do, he was only too

glad to make the dirt fly when Tom told him to dig for treasure under a pawpaw tree — while Tom sat nearby, comfortably smoking his pipe. At dawn, having found no golden horde of stolen coins, Sam staggered home exhausted, yet when the next whistle came, out he scrambled to dig in another place that Tom allowed was sure to be the right one.

Sam was a great one for what he called a joke, and one time his joke came close to tragedy. The boys enjoyed rolling stones down steep Holliday's Hill in front of a wagon, or a rider, who might be passing along the road below. The game was to scare the passer-by without getting caught by the patrol, whose duty it was to maintain order in town and on the road and to keep the slaves within bounds. One Sunday Sam, Will, and John picked out a huge boulder to roll. They worked and sweated and dug in turns, intending to send it crashing down, though not too close to anyone. Somebody miscalculated.

"Look out! She's a-rolling!"

John leaped from the hole, and the boulder roared and crashed down the hill. At that moment a Negro man had the bad luck to be driving past the spot. As his frightened eyes turned upward the stone bounced completely over his wagon without touching it, and landed on the other side.

That was the last time Sam ever rolled a stone. He and his friends hid from the patrol. And that evening when a resounding thunderstorm swept in over the river, to rip the heavens with bolt after bolt of lightning, Sam pulled covers over his head in bed and made a promise to lead a better life.

Sam had been told, time and again, that he would be struck by lightning if he didn't behave better. Wasn't that solemn warning given all of the worshipers in the Presbyterian Church attended, though reluctantly, by young Sam? Every time a storm broke Sam turned pale and thought that the bolt was directed at him. His remorse lasted until next morning. When the sun shone forgivingly and no fury remained in the heavens, Sam decided that it would do no harm to play hooky and go with Tom to explore the caves again.

The miles of cave passages winding through the cliffs overlooking the river never lost their scary fascination. Sam was once lost in the caves after a picnic, along with his little sweetheart, Laura Hawkins, and the terror that he felt when he caught a glimpse of a murderer known as Injun Joe gave him nightmares for months.

Sam saw other things that gave him nightmares too. In a village on the frontier life was fun, but it could be suddenly frightening. Although Hannibal was part of the South, and some of its people owned a few household and farm slaves, it did not have a plantation society. Immigrants going into the West came continuously through the town, and it did not have the settled life of the South before the war. Sight of death was not unusual, even for children. Once Sam saw his quiet father, not naturally a violent man, stop a street fight by hitting one of the men with a stone cutter's mallet.

And when he was a young child Sam had seen a man shot down in cold blood on the plank sidewalks of Hannibal. So he was used to violence, and he learned to hate it early. One night he came home from a forbidden trip a little way down-river in a rowboat "borrowed" for the occasion. Sam's conscience was not exactly hurting him, but he thought that maybe he would do well to remain away from his mother's watchful eye until morning, when there would be no time to talk to him. So Sam went to his father's office and crawled in through a window. He curled up on a horsehair sofa and went to sleep.

After a time he awakened, strangely uneasy. His eyes opened to see a shaft of moonlight touching a figure stretched out on the floor. Sam sat up and took a better look. It was the body of a man murdered that day on the street, put here until the undertaker could come for him. Sam could see a bullet hole in his head. He described afterwards how he went out of the place. "I do not say that I went in a hurry, but I simply went out of the window, and I carried the sash with me. I did not need the window sash, but it was easier to take it than to leave it, and so I took it. I was not scared, but I was considerably agitated."

Sam's friends in town included the Negroes, both slaves and freedmen. To him slavery was just a fact, like the flowing river and the town — like the one-room jail, where he and Tom

16

Blankenship took matches and food to pass through the barred window to a tramp — like gunfights in the street — like the school and the church and the caves. This was Hannibal, Missouri, before the Civil War. This was Sam's world. Yet there were things about it that he didn't like even as a child, and they made him wonder how such things could come to be.

Sam saw slaves chained together being taken down the river for sale. This was the way it was. He once saw his just and kind father whip Jenny, their slave girl, because she had been impudent to her mistress. Mrs. Clemens, who had great sympathy for the troubles of slaves, accepted the fact of slavery, and it was she who had asked her husband to punish Jenny. Later, when Jenny was sold because the family hadn't the income to keep her and needed the money that she would bring, they hired a little slave boy named Sandy to help with the chores a few hours a week. Sandy had a habit of singing the same song over and over, much to everybody's annoyance. Once Sam asked his mother to make Sandy stop singing — it was awful to hear it so much. Jane Clemens replied sadly, "Sandy is far from his family, and will never see them again. When he sings it shows maybe he is not remembering. When he stops I can't bear it."

As Sam grew he became a fine judge of his mother's moods, and expert in circumventing her wrath. She believed that she could always detect his circumventions — but he had a rather low opinion of her skill. Yet his admiration for her courage and character knew no bounds. Once he watched her deliberately stand before a terrified girl, whose wild, drunken father was threatening her with a knife. Jane Clemens gave the man a tongue lashing that caused him to drop his weapon and go away in silence.

"Sam," he could often hear his mother call, "Sam!" No answer. "What's gone with that boy, I wonder? You, SAM!"

He could hear her, for he was hiding nearby, but he made it a rule never to show himself until that, "You, SAM!" came ringing out. Then he went in a hurry. That meant business.

The Adventures of Tom Sawyer are the boy adventures of Sam Clemens, although the story is imaginary. Most of the names are different, and somehow the story changed into fiction, for Mark Twain combined the adventures of his friends with his own, and so wove his plot into a pattern of interest and excitement. Cardiff Hill was really Holliday's Hill, and Sam Clemens became Tom Sawyer. Tom Blankenship, that hero of his boyhood, turned into Huckleberry Finn. Between the covers of this book Sam put his memories of the caves, his friends, his sweethearts, his sister, and brother Henry, Injun Joe, the village of Hannibal, and the great wide-spreading river. And Jane Clemens is there too, for she is the Aunt Polly of *The Adventures of Tom Sawyer*.

The Adventures of
TOM SAWYER

Spring had come to St. Petersburg, Missouri, bringing a smile to even the grimmest winter face. Yet Tom Sawyer was downhearted. His Aunt Polly had caught him playing hookey from school the day before, and so today he must whitewash the fence. It was Saturday morning, just right for fishing or watching a steamboat edge in to the river landing. And then, "at this dark and hopeless moment an inspiration burst upon him." Tom's inspirations were not only original, they were successful too, and hilariously funny as well.

There was a newcomer in town. She was Becky Thatcher, whose golden braids and blue eyes were the envy of girls and the admiration of boys. Which boy would she notice? Tom Sawyer put on a campaign to achieve that honor, which he felt would be well deserved. Forthcoming events placed an awful strain on him, yet he was ready to prove his devotion at all times, even if he died doing it.

Aunt Polly told Tom not to play with Huckleberry Finn because he wasn't respectable. But, since Huck was the only boy who could live as he pleased, and knew more exciting things than all the other boys put together, Tom became Huck's friend. He even went with Huck to the graveyard to learn how to cure warts. Instead, the boys were cured of going to the graveyard, for that night they were the only witnesses to a horrible murder. Now Tom and Huck had a dangerous secret to keep, and trying to keep it scared them nearly to death.

A time came when life at home, in school, and in Sunday school wasn't worth shucks to Tom Sawyer. He felt that he was blamed for everything bad that happened in the town. So Tom persuaded Huck and Joe Harper to run away with him to a big wooded island. For a while they led a wonderful life. Then things began to happen, and it was up to Tom to think of some fancy escapades and schemes to solve their problems. That wasn't too difficult for the most ingenious boy on the Mississippi, and the results were surprising.

The sleepy town of St. Petersburg was shaken awake by the murder trial of old Muff Potter, who could remember nothing of that night in the graveyard. Tom and Huck knew who the murderer was, but they were afraid to break their vow of secrecy. Finally Tom realized that he had to stand up and tell the truth. That made him a hero all right, but he couldn't find much glory in it, for he knew that the murderer was still at large.

Of all the events of the year Tom and his friends looked forward most to a big summer picnic near a vast and mysterious cave. This party always ended with an exploration of some of the cave passages. Tom and Becky, wandering deeper and deeper, and farther and farther from the others, became lost. It took all of Tom's courage to face the dangers in the cave, and to try to rescue Becky. People thought well of him because of the way he did both. And they thought so much of Huck Finn, too, that a kind widow took him into her home to live.

2

When in Doubt — Do It!

SAM HAD TRIED hard to persuade his mother to let him leave school. He left the reading to Henry, and if he wanted to know anything from a book he just asked his brother. From the age of eleven on Sam had various odd jobs that brought in some small financial help to the family.

John Marshall Clemens was suddenly taken ill with pneumonia and lived only a short time afterwards. He left his wife and children without means of support, dazed with grief and shock. Sam, sensitive and impulsive, loving and rebellious at the same time, was crushed by remembrance of his own constant careless disobedience of his father's wishes. Orion came home from St. Louis, where he was working as a typesetter on a newspaper, and the family considered ways of survival.

Orion could send home a part of his small wages. Pamela could teach piano and guitar, and Jane Clemens could take a few boarders. What about Sam?

A year later Jane and Orion decided that Sam must become a printer's apprentice. A Mr. Ament had just come to Hannibal and had bought the equipment of the defunct *Gazette,* the newspaper of the Democratic Party of the town, and set up his *Missouri Courier.* He agreed to take Sam to work, pay him with board and room, and to give him two suits of clothes a year.

At first Sam was the errand boy and printer's devil, carrying out these jobs outside school hours. Then it was discovered that he learned quickly, so he was taught the printing trade, and Sam's wish to leave school was granted when he was thirteen or fourteen years old. There was one other apprentice, as well as a journeyman printer living in the print shop, and the three had fine times together. Sam was the smallest, the other apprentice was a giant of a boy. Ament gave them his own cast-off clothing. Sam was swallowed up in them, and had to set type standing on a box with his sleeves and trousers turned up "to his ears," as he put it, while the other boy could scarcely sit down for fear that he would split his skin-tight breeches.

Cigars were cheap, and all Hannibal boys learned to smoke at about the age of nine or so. Sam had a strong cigar or a corn-cob pipe hanging from the corner of his mouth as he worked. He put it down when he wanted to sing a comic song, and he was always ready to lay it aside, assume that innocent look, and play a joke on somebody.

Since he usually finished about three in the afternoon, there was still time for adventures on Holliday's Hill, in the cave, the creek, and on the river. But for all the jokes, and the free roaming life with his friends after work, Sam was leading a hard life now. Mr. Ament gave him mighty little to eat. The boys had to sleep on quilts on the floor of the printing office but they felt that they had a right to steal down cellar at night, bring up apples, onions, and potatoes and cook them on the office heating stove.

A year after his apprenticeship began Sam was the standby of the newspaper office. He became a first-class typesetter. He worked well, and he read all of the copy that came into the office, since nobody forced him to do it. He could run the job-press

and sing at the same time. He delivered the papers. He made no money, but by the time he was fifteen he was acting as sub-editor. He still enlivened any place where he happened to be. One fine summer's day Sam, looking out of the window, had to make a split-second decision. Would he eat the luscious ripe piece of watermelon in his hand, or would he drop it on the unsuspecting head of his brother Henry, who was walking past the print shop? Sam never hesitated at a crucial time like that. His motto was "When in doubt — do it!" He did. The sight of his brother crowned with watermelon was sufficient compensation for its loss to Sam.

Sam was on hand for every excitement. When the circus came to Hannibal he was there, and he sat in the front row at the minstrel show. Sam went to see the hypnotist perform, and volunteered as a subject. He gave the crowd a wild performance, and afterwards said that it was all an act on his part, although his mother and Orion always insisted that Sam was really hypnotized. He carried Laura Hawkins' skates when a winter crowd went to the frozen river, and he gallantly held her basket of lunch at the summer picnics.

One day Sam was hungry and feeling miserable. He was a boy of rapidly shifting moods, and his troubles were many. He was going home from the newspaper office. A strong wind blew through his thin jacket. He bent his head into the blast, and suddenly saw a sheet of paper tossed at his feet. Sam picked it up and read it as he walked. It was a page torn from a book. No book had ever really interested Sam. This page was from the story of Joan of Arc. It caught his wild imagination, and his ready sympathy and compassion. He read it over and over. Then he went around borrowing all of the books that he could find, and plunged deep into the world of reading. Joan of Arc

became his favorite story. From this discovery there grew an enormous interest in all history, in all of the activity of mankind, and this interest was to remain with him for the rest of his life. To everybody's amazement, Sam began to thirst for knowledge. He even talked John Briggs and several other boys into joining him in a small class that he persuaded a German shoemaker to teach. Since the shoemaker knew little English this was not too hopeful a pursuit; yet it was here that Sam began to learn German, a language he later spoke well.

Everybody liked Sam, although he sometimes made them uncomfortably aware that they were ridiculous. He was strangely full of contradictions, rude and yet often considerate, rough, and often gentle, funny and sometimes very serious. He loved animals, particularly cats. Like his mother he felt at home with cats, and always had a favorite among them, a cat that invariably sat on a chair beside him when he had dinner at home. Sam could play pranks, and he could hate a bully, too.

Any injustice sent him into a raging, fighting fury, and so did cheating.

When Orion returned to Hannibal and got a loan that enabled him to buy one of the newspapers in the village, the Hannibal *Journal*, Sam went to work for him. Henry, two years younger, was put to learning typesetting after school. Sam moved back home. At this time he believed that his future was to become a journeyman printer, roaming about from one newspaper to another. He thought that such a life would be full of adventure and fun. Now, however, he was only fifteen and must stay at home to help Orion for a while.

A country boy named Jim Wolfe, green and bashful, came to room with Sam and learn the trade. One night Pamela gave a candy-pulling party. The boys were not invited, for they were too young, and so went up to bed. As they dropped off to sleep a fearful caterwauling began on the sloping roof outside the window. These sounds were mixed with laughter and conversation from the party, where at that moment pans of candy were placed to cool in the arbor built against the shed roof.

Jim Wolfe grew enraged at the cat fight, and muttered, "I'd like to knock those cats' heads together."

"Why don't you?" asked Sam. "You're scared to. I dare you!"

Jim got out of bed, pulled some knit stockings on his legs, and crawled out of the window into the snow. The roof sloped gently, and Jim had little trouble advancing on the cats, although it was very cold out there, and he in his night-shirt and stockings! Just as he got halfway down his feet struck a patch of ice and flew out from under him. The cats screeched and ran for cover. Sam, head out of window, howled

for joy as he saw Jim go crashing through the snow-covered arbor right down into the party guests and their pans of molasses candy!

The next day while he was eating gingerbread with the baker's son, Sam regaled him with "Jim Wolfe and the Tom Cats" and sent the boy off into peals of laughter. This was the first funny story that Sam Clemens ever told, and he went home pleased with himself. He had tasted the pleasure of realizing that he was a born storyteller.

Sam found that working for brother Orion had its problems. Orion was anxious to make his paper a success, and it seemed for a while that he could do it. He started well, wrote good editorials, and had a fine worker in Sam. Orion, however, was like his dreamy, impractical father, and was just as unsuccessful in business. He made mistakes, lost money, and the newspaper's popularity began to go. Now there were weeks when Sam received no pay, and Orion could not even give him two old suits to wear, for Orion had no extra clothing.

Sam worked well, but brother Henry was not much of a typesetter. Orion often made Sam stay late to do over the work that Henry had done so badly. This meant no more late afternoons in the woods and on the river with his friends. Sam boiled with anger over this injustice. One day he approached Orion with a request.

"I've found a good gun a man wants to sell cheap. I want a gun, Orion. Pay me some of the wages you owe so that I can buy it."

"How can I? I haven't the money. You know the paper isn't doing well. I just can't do it."

Sam was miserably unhappy; life seemed to stretch out

before him as nothing but hard work and no pleasure. He raged and swore, but Orion, usually gentle and accommodating, was desperate and unable to consider Sam at all. His mother worked hard too, taking in a few boarders again, while Pamela tried to get up another music class. Everything seemed against them. Disasters increased. A cow got into the printing office one night, knocked over a type case, and chewed up two rollers. This was followed by a fire in the office. Orion added on to the upstairs in their home, and, to save office rent, moved his remaining office gear and press into the first floor of the small house. Then Orion decided to go to Tennessee to try to sell what they had left of the almost worthless wild land that Judge Clemens had bought, believing it would secure their future. He left Sam in charge of the paper.

Sam was delighted. He said nothing to anybody and made up his mind to increase the circulation of the paper. He thought that he could spice it up a bit. He went about town gathering up all of the gossip that he heard, and then wrote it for the paper, with names and dates. This did please the populace — that is, all but those whose names appeared in the "spicy" stories. And it raised the circulation, all right.

Since nobody had much money at that time, most subscribers paid in produce. The office filled up with wormy turnips, ancient potatoes, and salty bacon. From time to time one of the subjects of the stories would show up, shotgun in hand. Then when he saw that the outrage had been perpetrated by a youth with innocent eyes and a suddenly assumed expression of stupidity, he went away sputtering, with the belief that the boy was simple-minded.

Sam then decided that the paper needed something a little more literary, something lofty in spirit, perhaps. He pub-

lished a sentimental poem, supposedly written by a farmer, although his friends believed that he was the author himself. And he put the title on it: —

LOVE CONCEALED
To Miss Katie of H——l.

Having created something of a sensation among the readers of the newspaper, Sam then thought up a feature calculated to top all others. In addition to the two newspapers there was now a third publishing in town, and a story was being whispered around about its editor. It seems that the unfortunate fellow had been disappointed in love. Unable to bear his sorrows, he arose from his bed one sleepless night, picked up a walking stick, and went down to Bear Creek, to drown himself. Sam wrote this story up in his lively style, with special emphasis on the ending, in which he told how the editor got out into the stream, changed his mind, and waded back to shore.

Now, as if stretching of the facts a little were not bad enough, Sam decided to embellish the story. He was always able to draw quite well, in cartoon style. He took two large

pieces of wooden display type, turned them over, and cut into the wood a picture of the editor in his nightshirt, a lantern in one hand, testing the depth of the river with his cane. This woodcut he inked and printed along with the story. Next day the editor charged into the *Journal* office like a rampaging buffalo, ready to tear his rival editor apart. Finding only a boy whose age made impossible the satisfaction of honor, he turned and fled. That night he left town, never to return.

Orion, however, did return. Sam thought his older brother the most ungrateful fellow he had ever seen, for the expanded subscription list and the great piles of produce did not interest him. He put Sam in his place again, as typesetter and printer, apologized to a long list of citizens, and nipped his young brother's writing career in the bud. If Orion did not appreciate the larger circulation, then neither did Sam appreciate the fact that Orion had saved him from jail — or destruction.

Nevertheless, this was a first sight of his own writing in print, and Sam liked the feeling it gave him. He wrote several humorous anecdotes and sent them to a paper in Philadelphia. He received no payment for them, but the fact that they were printed was enough. This filled him with a joy that was never exceeded by his pleasure in the publication of his works under the name of Mark Twain.

The Clemens family had a difficult life. The house was badly crowded with the newspaper office and press. Henry, who was good and gentle, remained a student, but not a good workman, and Sam continued to resent Orion's dictatorial treatment. His only pleasure was to slip off with his friends whenever he could get away — to stretch out on Glasscock's Island with Tom Blankenship, smoking and enjoying freedom for a few hours.

One cold spring day he and a friend decided to skate on the ice along the edge of the river for the last time before the final thaw. They miscalculated, though, and on their way back to shore, the ice broke suddenly. The river surged around them, grinding huge cakes of ice. The boys jumped from one piece of ice to another, wildly landing on their feet. Sam made it to shore, but his friend fell into the freezing water, was pulled out, and went home to have pneumonia, which left him with an ear infection that deafened him for life. Once again Sam felt responsible — since the idea of skating was his — and he thought that he had been spared "for hanging."

Orion's *Journal* continued to go down in quality. After a few years he could no longer pay his debts and the situation became desperate. Sam was eighteen years old then. By this time he knew as much, if not more, about editing a newspaper than his haphazard brother Orion did. It was time to break away and get out on his own. His sister Pamela was married to a Hannibal man who had become a merchant in St. Louis. Sam went to his mother and told her that he was going to St. Louis to stay with Pamela and get a job. He didn't tell her that his real desire was to see the world.

In June, 1853, Samuel Clemens boarded a riverboat for St. Louis, carrying all of his worldly goods under one arm. It was not a load to weigh him down.

Shortly after his departure Orion disposed of the *Journal*, moved to Muscatine, Iowa, and went to work for a printer. His mother and Henry moved with him. Sam worked for a few months in St. Louis, and then rode the bumpy, sooty, frightening, newly finished railroad to New York. He arrived there with a few dollars but soon found a job in the composing room of the *Evening News*.

Sam Clemens — country boy of Hannibal, Missouri, whose vision of the big city had been no larger than the sprawling, overgrown river town of St. Louis — walked the streets of New York City in a haze of excitement. He watched the elegant carriages of the rich spinning along cobblestone streets, proud footmen behind, uniformed coachmen in front, and inside he glimpsed the top-hatted gentlemen and the ladies in feathered bonnets. He looked at buildings all of five or six stories high. He halted suddenly at a clanging and a shouting, and felt the surge of power that the volunteer fire brigade generated — horses pounding, dogs running in front, and firemen in their red shirts racing their painted engines. Sam rubbed shoulders with the crowds — and never had he imagined that the world held so many people.

In New York Sam lived in a boardinghouse and had to walk two miles each way to work. He searched out books to read in the library, and spent most of his evenings there. He attended a play and saw the famous Edwin Forrest in *The Gladiator*.

After he had seen the sights of New York Sam grew restless

and went to Philadelphia. There he found work, lived in another boardinghouse, and after hours, as well as on Sundays, read, roamed the streets, and learned to know the old city. Sam wrote home that he liked Philadelphia better than New York, and that he had visited the grave of Benjamin Franklin. Like Franklin, Samuel Clemens had labored in his brother's printing shop, and had come to Philadelphia to seek his fortune. Unlike Franklin, he did not find it there.

Sam was lonely. Finally, he made a friend of an Englishman, who taught him how to grill a herring over a gas burner. Sam listened eagerly as his friend talked of philosophers whose names he had never heard. Alone in his room Sam wrote comic poetry and sent it to magazines, but none of it was accepted. When he had been away a year he suddenly realized that he was homesick.

One morning the Clemens family sat at breakfast in their home in Muscatine, Iowa. Orion owned a small job-printing plant, and so far was doing pretty well with it. The family heard footsteps on the porch, and looked up to see Sam standing in the doorway pointing a gun at them. He had traveled by train to St. Louis, sitting up for several days and nights in the sooty smoking cars, and had taken a boat from there.

"Orion," Sam said slowly, "you wouldn't let me buy a gun, so I bought one myself — and I'm going to use it now — in self-defense."

"Sam!" cried out Jane Clemens as she threw her arms around him. "You, SAM!"

A PREVIEW OF

The Adventures of

HUCKLEBERRY FINN

NOTICE

Persons attempting to find a motive in this narrative will be prosecuted; persons attempting to find a moral in it will be banished; persons attempting to find a plot in it will be shot.

BY ORDER OF THE AUTHOR,
Per G. G., Chief of Ordnance

Huck Finn realized that there were advantages in living with the widow and becoming "civilized." Nevertheless he often felt that he would gladly give them up if he could smoke his pipe, live in the open, and never have to do as he was told. He wouldn't have left on his own, but he had no choice when his mean old Pappy came to get him. When he got the chance he ran away from Pappy. In the Mississippi there were islands where a runaway with a fishline and gun could hide for a long time.

Huck soon found that there were others with the same idea. Miss Watson's slave Jim had also run away to the island, to avoid being sold down the river. Huck and Jim became friends and decided to look for freedom together in Illinois. They made a raft and slipped off downstream. They had to float by night and hide out by day. In spite of several narrow escapes from capture they enjoyed those nights, with the raft swinging along on the current and twinkling stars above.

And then somehow, in the darkness, the raft passed the limits of the free state, and Huck had to go ashore to find out where they were. He landed in the middle of a Southern feud, and managed to escape the general slaughter only by the skin of his teeth. Drifting downriver they knew that they were going deeper into slave territory, where dangers and troubles were many. Nevertheless they agreed to stick together.

As if there weren't troubles enough already for the runaways, more appeared with two strangers who invited themselves to the raft as passengers. They said their names were the "Duke of Bilgewater" and the "Rightful King of France," and it wasn't long before they had tricked Huck and Jim into becoming unwilling subjects.

They got Huck involved in more schemes for cheating and stealing
than he had ever heard of, and all down the Mississippi they had
to run for the raft just a fast jump ahead of the mobs. Not even
the revival meetings escaped the royal pair. Huck told Jim, "The
first thing I knew the King got a-going, and you could hear him
over everybody. Next he went a-charging up onto the platform,
and the preacher he begged him to speak to the people, and he
done it." Then Huck said that this had led to a passing of the
King's hat, with money jingling in for "the poor pirates of the Indian
Ocean." The runaways didn't know whether they were more
afraid of capture or of their passengers.

Although Huck and Jim stood by each other through all kinds of difficulties, they couldn't prevent Jim's capture at last. Huck was determined to try any plan to help him, but he was glad to see Tom Sawyer arrive with his own kind of ingenious plot. Events rushed on from trouble to danger, salted down with a dash of laughter. When everything was over, Huck was not too happy about his own prospects. "Aunt Sally, she's going to adopt me and sivilize me, and I can't stand it. I been there before."

3

King of the River

For a time Sam was glad to be back in the Mississippi Valley. When Orion, his wife, and Henry moved to Keokuk, Iowa, their mother went to live with Pamela. Once more Sam went to work for his older brother. He and Henry slept in the office on cots, and spent their evenings with several other young men who worked in the same building. Sam was supposed to make five dollars a week, a good wage for an expert typesetter, but, as in Hannibal, Orion was continually harassed by debts, and seldom paid his workmen. The young fellows had a rousing good time anyway, spending many an evening playing a guitar, singing funny songs, and swapping stories.

Reading at night after the others had gone to sleep became Sam's habit. He stretched out on his cot beside the printing press, lit a homemade Turkish water pipe, and burned the oil lamp until dawn. He read everything he could lay hands on, as if trying to educate himself now that he had passed beyond the walls of the log schoolhouse.

When he had been in Keokuk two years, Sam once more began to think of a change of scenery. There just seemed to be no future in working for Orion Clemens. Sam was twenty years old and in the mood for a new adventure when he hap-

pened on a book telling about recent explorations on the
Amazon River, in South America. His head became so full of
the stories of potential riches in cocoa that he could scarcely
sleep for wanting to go there. He would have boarded the
next riverboat had he had the fare, but when he pulled his
pockets out he found them as bare of riches as a barefoot yard
dog.

The chances of getting to South America seemed slim in-
deed one cold and windy November day. Sam was walking
down a Keokuk street, head bowed against the icy blast, hands
in pockets. A piece of green paper blew against his foot, and
seemed to stick there. Sam reached down for it, feeling oddly
excited. Amazed, his eyes fell on a fifty-dollar bill. He had
never even seen one before. This would pay his way to the
Amazon, or at least part of it. He would come home rolling
in wealth made from cocoa beans. Sam went back to the shop
and hid the bill in the lining of his coat, mentioning it to no
one. He could start right now. What was he waiting for? His
conscience must be holding him back, for it told him that

somebody else owned that money, that he should advertise it in the newspaper.

Telling about this experience, he said, "I didn't describe it very particularly, and I waited in daily fear that the owner would turn up and take away my good fortune. After a while I couldn't stand it any longer. I felt that I must take that fifty-dollar bill out of danger."

So Sam booked passage on a steamboat. He arrived in Cincinnati in November and stayed there until April, working as a printer, trying to save enough money to get to South America.

With spring there came a renewed urge to go to the Amazon River to find a fortune in cocoa beans, and so Sam, who had saved enough money for his passage from Cincinnati to New Orleans, boarded a packet. Sam was impulsive by nature, and often took action before he reflected. He said that when his actions got him into trouble people miles away could hear him reflecting on his foolishness.

The packet was called the *Paul Jones,* and Sam was as familiar with a steamboat as any of the boys who lived along the mighty river. He leaned on the railing as the gangplank came in, bells clanging, whistle blowing. The small steamboat swung out to midstream. It chugged downriver, skirting green islands, riding sandbars covered with muddy water, and pulling in from time to time beside a wharf to let passengers on and to load and unload bales of goods.

The language of the Mississippi rang in Sam Clemens' ears — the voice of the leadsman as he sounded the depths of the river with his lead and twine, striking three fathoms: "Mark — three!" Then "Quarter less three! . . . Half twain — quarter twain!" And at last the long, singing cry — for a depth of two fathoms of muddy Mississippi water — "M-a-r-k twain! M-a-r-k twain!"

Negro deckhands sang and the breeze rose with smell of bush and vine and tree. In early evening the moon came sailing into the sky to make a silver path for the little steamboat to follow.

Impulse hit Sam, and the ambition of his childhood rose to the surface. He forgot the Amazon and those rich cocoa beans. He felt that he had come home to his river and that only the Mississippi would ever suit him.

Sam thought that he knew perfectly well how big a task he was undertaking when he climbed into the pilot house, greeted Horace Bixby, the pilot, and asked, "How would you like a pilot to learn the river?"

"I wouldn't. Cub pilots are more trouble than they are worth."

All of the glory of the pilot shone around this Mr. Horace Bixby, of honest, forthright look and speech. Sam brought up every piece of persuasive artillery in his vocabulary and turned

it loose on Mr. Bixby. He told how much he knew of the river from living in Hannibal. He mentioned friends who had become river pilots, including the Bowen boys, whom Bixby knew and respected. It took three days of solid talking, but Sam won out. It would take money, though. Sam had his savings, and he knew that he could borrow a hundred dollars from Pamela's husband, Mr. Moffett. He promised to pay the rest of his tuition after he became a pilot. A pilot made a large salary and had few expenses. Sam drew a breath of pure unadulterated joy when Horace Bixby reluctantly agreed to take him on.

Writing about this moment later, Sam said, "I entered upon the small enterprise of 'learning' twelve or thirteen hundred miles of the great Mississippi River with the easy confidence of my time of life. If I had really known what I was about to require of my faculties, I should not have had the courage to begin. I supposed that all a pilot had to do was to keep his boat in the river and I did not consider that that could be much of a trick, since it was so wide."

Some of this was Mark Twain exaggeration, to make a good story, but Sam Clemens knew that the learning job would take every ounce of his mental capacity. In those days, before the Civil War, it took twenty-five days to load and unload cargo and take the steamboat from St. Louis to New Orleans and back. Wages for a licensed pilot came to $250 a month, an enormous sum for that time. The Pilots' Association kept wages up and controlled the river traffic completely. Any pilot had power and commanded respect. He was king of the river and could even tell the captain what to do. A cub was lucky to be the pupil of a good pilot, and Horace Bixby ranked at the very top.

Bixby could blow up suddenly like a steamboat with an overloaded boiler, yet he was a kindly man as well as a stern one. If he taught a cub, that cub had to be a credit to his teacher. When Sam forgot the thousands of points, islands, shoals, bars, snags, and landmarks on the huge river, Bixby lit into him full blast. Then he simmered down, and gently told the cub to get a notebook and put down every smallest item of knowledge. When Sam thought that he had memorized everything in sight, Bixby turned on him and told him that he had only just begun to learn this river. Sam believed him, for he had watched Mr. Bixby put the *Paul Jones* over a line of dangerous reefs and bring her through with a skill that left the others in the pilothouse gasping, "By the Shadow of Death, but he's a lightning pilot!" No higher compliment could be paid a pilot by his fellow rivermen. Sam could not have found a better teacher.

Sam had to learn the shape of the mighty stream, and he had to know it so well that in the dark, without stars or moon, he could "feel" the shape of the river, just as he "felt" the shape of his own hallway at home. Then, when Sam thought he had worn his brain to rags learning these thousands of details by heart, Bixby told him that moonlight was even worse than total darkness. The glint of light on shoals and bars and snags and riffles was deceptive and the cub had to know what every dimple in the water meant.

Sam struggled and swore and enjoyed it all enormously. He learned about other things also — the varied and exciting kinds of people traveling the steamboats, and something about exotic New Orleans. Living on the river gave him a taste of every kind of humanity there was — and Sam Clemens wasn't the kind to forget anything that he learned.

After months with Mr. Bixby, Sam was transferred for a time to another steamboat, the *Pennsylvania*. Learning that his brother Henry wanted to work on the river, Sam got him a job on his boat. In spite of their battles as children, these two brothers were now devoted to each other.

One day the pilot on the *Pennsylvania*, a brutal fellow, attacked Henry Clemens for some minor slip, and Sam hit his superior with a chair. As a result Sam was laid off of the ship for one trip. On this very trip upstream the *Pennsylvania* exploded and 150 people were killed or injured. When Sam arrived at the town to which the injured had been taken, Henry was dying. He took his younger brother home to be buried beside his father. Because he had arranged to put Henry on board, Sam blamed himself for the tragedy, and it was a grief to him as long as he lived.

Sam became a pilot, and he was a good one. For four years he guided his steamboats along the river, and for these four years he was a king, and a good deal happier than most monarchs. It was about this time that Sam, pretty cocky as a pilot on the river, could not resist playing one of his jokes in print.

A humorless but respected old pilot named Sellers often sent solemn letters to the New Orleans newspapers, telling of the condition of the river. ·He signed some of them "Mark Twain." Now Sam Clemens was inspired to write a take-off on them. It wasn't signed "Mark Twain," or Sellers, of course, but the tone of the originals was so well imitated, and it was so absurd, that the pilots all roared with laughter. Sam enjoyed the fun too, until he realized that the old man was so hurt and humiliated that he would never again write a letter. Sam did not forgive himself for being so thoughtless.

Life on the river suited Sam, and he intended to remain a

pilot to the end of his days. Then events gave a twist and a turn once more — and this twist was a major catastrophe and upheaval for the whole country. Fort Sumter was fired on, and civil war, long smoldering, burst into flames. Like a great many other people living in a state bordering the North, Sam Clemens of Hannibal, Missouri, found it hard to decide where his loyalty lay. Some pilots were going into military service to keep steamboats on the river for the use of the Union Army, but Sam thought it too dangerous up there in the glass pilothouse with guns booming away. He went to St. Louis to visit his mother and sister for a few days, and then to Hannibal to see his old friends. Orion, living in Keokuk, Iowa, was forthrightly against slavery. Sam was inclined that way himself, and yet he did not feel so strongly about it that he wished to enter the Union Army.

In Hannibal his friends convinced him that the Confederacy was the right cause, that the whole South was in danger, and that he must join with them to repel the invader. It was difficult to know which army might do the invading, since Missouri had sympathizers on both sides, but Sam made up his mind to be a Confederate soldier. He joined a little group of fourteen men who planned to search for the Confederate Army.

Their first camp was made in farming country. Confederate sympathizers among the farmers provided them with provisions and horses of a rather nondescript sort. Sam was given a small yellow mule called Paint Brush, and he couldn't help but realize that he created an odd appearance as he rode the mule with his military gear tied all around his saddle. His gear consisted of an old rifle, blankets, a frying pan, a small suitcase, a homemade quilt, an extra pair of cowskin boots, a coil of rope, and an umbrella.

The "battalion" rode to Salt River and encamped near Florida, the crossroads village where Sam had spent happy summers on his uncle's farm. There they elected officers.

Nobody in the group knew anything about military training, and, since the "battalion" was so small the election of officers left only three privates. This annoyed the privates, and they refused point-blank to obey orders. Sam was voted second lieutenant, but he was baffled when he ordered Sam Bowen to serve as a picket, and Bowen refused to do it. Threatening him with court-martial and death by firing squad only sent him out into the sun to sit on a log and swear; and then to stretch out on the ground and go to sleep. There seemed to be nothing that Lieutenant Clemens could do about it, except to hope that no enemy would pull into sight.

Sam's chief trouble was the mule Paint Brush. As he described it in "The Private History of a Campaign That Failed":

The creature that fell to my share was a very small mule, and yet so quick and active that it could throw me without difficulty; and it did this whenever I got on it. Then it would bray — stretching its neck

out, laying its ears back, and spreading its jaws till you could see down to its works. It was a disagreeable animal, in every way. If I took it by the bridle and tried to lead it off the grounds, it would sit down and brace back, and no one could budge it. However, I was not entirely destitute of military resources, and I did presently manage to spoil this game; for I had seen many a steamboat aground in my time, and knew a trick or two which even a grounded mule would be obliged to respect. There was a well by the corn-crib; so I substituted thirty fathom of rope for the bridle, and fetched him home with the windlass.

There had been no sign of the enemy so far, and no indication that these new recruits were approaching the Confederate Army. Troubles multiplied. Sam developed a boil and had to lie in the hay in a farmer's barn loft while his companions scouted the vicinity. The "battalion" was thoroughly confused by the whole march.

At last they arrived at a farm owned by a Confederate colonel. It was late at night and the farmhouse was unlighted. The troops decided to sleep in the barn and not disturb the family. One of the soldiers lit up his pipe for a last smoke, and then laid it down in the hay. Sam, drifting off to sleep, was awakened by a cry of "Fire!"

The smell of smoke was strong, and the hay was blazing all around him. Twisting suddenly away from it, Sam rolled out of the open loft door and descended abruptly into the barnyard. Before he could get up his excited friends pitched the blazing hay out of the loft on top of him. Sam leaped out of the fire, using language that was hotter than the blaze. And in the fall he had sprained his ankle. The colonel's wife put him to bed in the farmhouse and took care of him. When in the morning the "battalion" marched away, Sam bade his fellow soldiers and Paint Brush farewell without regrets. He concluded that he had had enough of war, and would go to Keokuk to see his brother. Perhaps Orion would welcome him, even if he had been a Confederate soldier for all-too-lively, though unwarlike, weeks.

For the first time the Clemens family really believed that Orion might be a success. Prospects were good. He had campaigned for Abraham Lincoln in the recent election, and was known to the Iowa Republicans as an antislavery man. This resulted in an appointment as secretary to the new governor of Nevada Territory. Orion had a job now — but no money yet. When Sam arrived with several hundred dollars saved from his piloting days, Orion suggested that Sam go along to Nevada as his secretary, and that Sam pay the fare west for both of them. So Sam put his longing regret for piloting days out of mind, equipped himself with a small pistol, heavy clothing, a couple of blankets, and a Western hat. He was ready for Indians, buffaloes, the Great Plains, and the mighty Rockies!

This book is, in part, the joyful tale of how young Sam Clemens became a pilot on the Mississippi, and of how he "learned the river" the hard way. It is also the story of the great muddy stream itself, dividing a continent, shifting as it flows between wooded banks. First it was the home of Indian tribes, hunting on its shores and moving on its currents in light canoes. Then came French and Spanish explorers to claim it for distant kings. In the last section Mark Twain writes of a return visit to the river twenty years later, of the changes that he found there, and of his pleasure in renewing memories of a period which he always called the happiest time of his life.

Many years after the explorers had come and gone, barges, keelboats, broadhorns and rafts began to float cargoes downriver. Steamboatmen looked with contempt on these wild, rafting fellows, who howled, "I'm the man they call Sudden Death and Desolation! Whoop! Stand back and give me room," or "I'm a Child of Calamity and spoiling for a fight!" Sam said that when he was a boy in Hannibal he and his friends would swim a quarter of a mile to crawl on a raft and get a ride,—and it was worth it, too.

A steamboat race on the river was a sight to bring every human being to the banks at a fast run. In New Orleans bands played, crowds cheered, smoke poured from stacks, crews sang and the forecastles were lit by a red glare from flaming torch baskets. Guns boomed out. The steamboats were off! They moved upriver side by side until one pulled gradually ahead. Every race was dangerous, and it took the most daring and expert pilot, captain and crew, risking destruction all the way, to bring their vessel in to a triumphant finish.

The Mississippi River was marked by famous spots, each one a jumping off place for a story. Strangers hung over the guard rails to stare at them as the ship's officers or passengers who lived on the river pointed out islands, points and villages where history had been made. This was the scene of a famous steamboat explosion. That was a town once far inland, but now, with the shifting of the erratic stream, a river landing. The most popular sight of all was an island, the onetime stronghold of the infamous Murrell and his gang of a thousand slave-stealers, robbers and cutthroats.

In New Orleans by mid-afternoon steamboats were tied up along the waterfront for a distance of three miles. Stacks smoked with burning pine, flags flew, mates swore, barrels, boxes and bales were swung on board. Passengers pushed to the landing stages, and drays and carriages were lined up on the narrow streets for blocks. Down the row of steamboats bells rang and whistles blew for sailing time. As Mark Twain remembered all of his life, "Steamer after steamer falls into line, and the stately procession goes winging its flight up the river."

4

Wild and Western

Hi-ya! G'lang," shouted the stagedriver.

Sam Clemens, stretched out on the pile of mail sacks, lit his pipe and sniffed the sagebrush-scented wind. Beside him, his brother Orion eased over his lanky frame to avoid the sharp corners of the unabridged dictionary that Sam had insisted on bringing along. As the stagecoach jolted and rocked and rattled across the prairies, plains, desert and into the hills, Sam felt as free as one of the unpleasant coyotes that he saw now and then. For once he thought that he had a workable arrangement with Orion; his brother had the job and Sam was supplying the money to get to it. Now and then he could feel the bag of three hundred silver dollars — the money he had left after the fare west had been paid — jolting against his back in the crevice between mail sacks where he kept it.

Every ten miles the stage drew up with a rush and a yell, and a flourish, before a way station. The flourish was pretty well wasted because the station was merely an adobe mud-brick building, where they changed horses, had a meal, and slept at night. Arrangements there were not elegant. After washing up in a tin basin with no towel, they ate salt bacon and beans.

As they rode along, the driver talked to the conductor who sat beside him. He described an Indian fight on his last trip or mentioned the notorious bad man of the West — Slade. Sam

listened to the gory tales and felt uneasily for his pistol at his belt.

Kansas! Nebraska! They rattled along, out of the United States, across the Little Blue and the Sandy Rivers, no more than muddy creeks to Sam Clemens, the Mississippi River pilot. Five hundred miles out and they began to peer ahead for a glimpse of a Pony Express Rider. Swapping horses at the relay stations as fast as they could leap from one to another, the pony riders swept along with their mailbags, covering 1900 miles from Sacramento, California, to St. Joseph, Missouri.

"Here one comes!" roared the driver. A tiny ball of dust appeared on the horizon. Pounding hoofs of the racing horse, a tiny figure in lightweight clothing, bent low on the stripped saddle, mailbags flapping. "Whoopee!" yelled Sam. Everybody

waved wildly. A flash of the hand, dust in the eyes — horse and rider disappeared like a puff of smoke in the distance.

"We're in Injun country now," growled out the driver. "We're coming into the Black Hills. Alongside of you there's a bullet hole from the last trip. Got it about this region. But it's not as bad as the run I used to have down where Apaches annoyed me so I nearly about starved to death. They put me so full of holes I couldn't hold my vittles."

They rattled into Salt Lake City, where Brigham Young ran the only independent country on the continent, outside of the United States. He kept his large family of wives and children in the Lion's House in the center of the town. Sam had heard a lot about the Mormon Avenging Angel army, but found the one angel member he met to be only a rough man with a gun.

Off again after a rest, through thick white alkali desert, up into mountains, climbing. On the twentieth day out from Missouri they saw ahead of them, covered with alkali dust, set among sagebrush and greasewood bushes, the town of Carson City, capital of Nevada Territory. It was a small bunch of flimsy houses in the shadow of high mountains, but to Sam Clemens — printer, newspaperman, river pilot — it was high adventure.

They jumped down at the town square, packed with wagons and horses, oxen, and mules. In the streets dust rose in clouds and settled again on broad-brimmed hats and bearded faces. At two o'clock every afternoon the powerful wind, the "Washoe zephyr" blew. In all this flat plain under the frowning mountains there was not a tree, bush, or flower, except for the sage and greasewood of the desert. The wind swept violently down, and Sam claimed when it did that he could see nothing but a huge cloud overhead with layers of flying objects — hats, parasols, chickens, children, roofs, sheds, and mules. Mules were called "Washoe canaries." Their bray could be heard by day and by night in this country known locally as "Washoe."

Sam moved with thirteen other men into a second-floor room of a boardinghouse run by a lady named Mrs. Murphy. Orion, by virtue of his position as secretary to the governor, had a corner of a room to himself downstairs. Sam's promised job with his brother soon proved to be nonexistent, but this didn't bother him much. He still had some money. Sam's thirteen rowdy roommates had come out West with the new governor. The governor called them his "brigade" but the only work that he could think up for them to do was surveying out on the desert. He said he hoped to survey them into Utah and out of his jurisdiction — and then telegraph Brigham Young to hang them for trespass.

While the brigade was out of work, they all amused themselves collecting tarantulas, which they lined up on a long shelf under water glasses. One night the Washoe zephyr blew so hard that the roof of a stable next door crashed into the room, and brought down the shelf. A wild cry rang out in the dark where fourteen men were sleeping.

"Tarantulas is loose!"

All fourteen leaped up and crouched down on the beds, expecting the hairy, monstrous insects to attack. The only sound heard was a chorus of hoarse breathing — then a shout.

"He's got me! I'm dead. Fetch a lantern."

Mrs. Murphy loomed up in the doorway with a light, and saw the men frozen into strange attitudes. The fellow who had been "bitten" held up a finger pinched by a trunk lid. All tarantulas had disappeared, probably scared to death by the brigade, and were never seen again.

Sam took a vacation from doing nothing in Carson City, and spent several fine weeks with a friend camping at lovely Lake Tahoe over the mountains. The boys staked out a timber claim there. When they watched their claim go up in fire and smoke because they had been careless about a campfire, they came mournfully back. Sam was footloose again.

Then he bought a horse — a genuine Mexican plug — and thought that he would go prospecting. This plug had other ideas. When Sam had been bucked to the ground six times in rapid succession he gave the beast to a gullible passing immigrant. Everybody was out silver mining, and the "boom" brought men on foot, horse, mule, wagon, and by stage. Riches in silver were found daily. Nobody talked anything but mining. It was a strike found at the Orphir Mine, or the Gould & Curry,

71

the Bald Eagle, the Mary Ann, the Lady Franklin, or the Rough
and Ready, the Esmeralda, or the Humboldt. Wagons filled
with quartz or loads of silver brick filed through Carson City.

Sam was running a high "silver fever" himself by now, and so
he took to the hills with pick and shovel, making for the Humboldt. He joined three friends and walked for fifteen days to a
steep canyon. There they dug and peered, day after day. Sam,
the greenhorn, yelled excitedly when he found a few glittering
particles which he took for gold. One partner was an old pros-
pector. He looked disgusted. "Gold? That's nothing but fool's
gold — worthless iron pyrites — that's all."

Discouraged by the Humboldt, Sam returned to Carson City
and made friends with a miner named Calvin H. Higbe. About
that time a new sensation hit the town, and the Wild West Mine
was the only subject of excited conversation. It was located near
a mining town called Esmeralda, and this was its second boom.
Higbe knew that the rich ore was coming into the mine from a
hidden vein leading into it from an adjoining area. The Wild

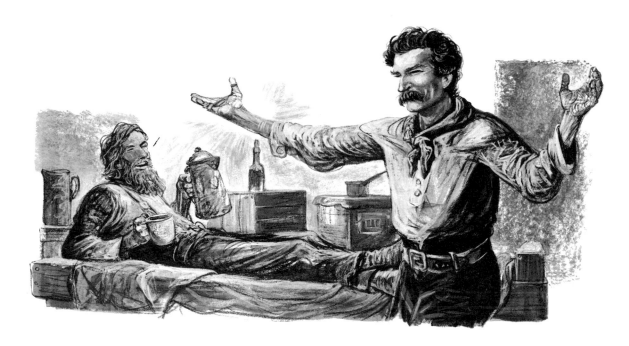

West Mine would be worthless without the piece of land next to it. Higbe and Clemens put in a claim to the piece.

A strike! A rich vein. A bonanza! Sam and Higbe planned a trip east as millionaires — traveling like nabobs. Then Sam's luck shifted, as was its habit. The claim had to be worked by a certain date, or it was lost by default. Sam was called out of town to nurse a sick friend, counting on Higbe to work the claim. But Higbe took a trip because he thought that Sam was working the claim. When Sam returned he found that the claim had lapsed and he and Higbe had to watch others get rich on it.

Sam went to work at hard labor in a quartz mill and at the end of an exhausted week he had not made enough to pay for room and board. Yet he found the energy, from time to time, to write a short descriptive letter or funny story for a newspaper. He sent them to the *Daily Territorial Enterprise*, at Virginia City, another Nevada boom town, and it cheered him to see them in print.

One day he joined the line at the post office and was surprised to receive a letter from Virginia City. The *Enterprise* wanted Sam Clemens to come there at once to take a job as city editor at a salary of twenty-five dollars a week. This would be the first time that he would have a job as a journalist and not a typesetter. They wanted him to be an editor! He started for Virginia City that day.

Joe Goodman, of the *Enterprise,* looked up to see his new sub-editor standing in the doorway — slouch hat, red whiskers, blue woolen shirt, pants stuffed into boots, and a navy revolver slung from his belt. He welcomed Sam, put him to work, and found a place for him to sleep.

Sam soon bought clothing that was a little better suited to Virginia City and his position as a newspaperman. He felt right at home there, for this was a wilder, larger, dustier, more rip-snorting and roaring mining city than the one that he had just left. He joined the other reporters out gathering news in the streets, saloons, gambling palaces — from fire companies, hotels, the theater, and the jail. News was lively enough, for there was a duel or a shooting fray on the street nearly every day, and when the normal flow of news seemed a bit slow, Sam added touches of his own to give it interest.

Virginia City was perched partway up a high mountain, more than 7000 feet above sea level. Wooden buildings were going up all of the time, the noise of hammering and sawing joining the sound of wagon wheels, braying mules and donkeys, yells and songs. Underground a maze of tunnels was dug directly below the city itself, for the rich Comstock lode ran there. Sam often felt his office chair jolt as a blast of dynamite went off below.

Sam Clemens was a good reporter, and it wasn't long before his salary was raised to forty dollars a week. Yet in his thoughts this was the smallest part of his "wealth." Mining stock was

issued as so many "feet" in a mine. Sam and his *Enterprise* cronies never stepped out on the rattling plank sidewalk without having some miner give them a few feet in a new mine — expecting in return a notice of the strike in the columns of the papers.

"Whoopee! She's in. Biggest, richest strike ever seen. A few feet for you, Mr. Clemens — hope you will say a little — in tomorrow's *Enterprise* —"

Sam had a trunkful of mining stock, most of it worthless. Every little shaft into the earth would make a million. Each handful of rock was richer than the last. There wasn't a poor man in Virginia City — at least in hope. Every little wildcat mine was a-coming in strong! And if expectation failed for a claim, the owner often "salted" it with a judicious handful of good rich ore, and arranged to sell it to a sucker.

The city editor of the *Enterprise* was also a "legman" reporter, for the newspaper staff was so small that at first they slept in the one room where the press and office were located. Any day Sam could see a murder, or hear of one. The busiest place around seemed to be the cemetery, otherwise known as Boot

Hill, for the men who died with their boots on. Sam was told that the first twenty-six graves were occupied by murdered men. He took a resolution then and there that he would leave his revolver peacefully at home — and hold himself down to merely reporting a hot quarrel. The most respected men walking the streets were not bankers, doctors, lawyers, and ministers. They were the "bad men" — gunslingers, fast on the draw.

East of the Mississippi the great war was on, with North fighting South. In the border states such as Missouri, often brother against brother, or father against son. On this high mountain in Nevada one scarcely knew that blood was flowing in the East — not from the talk or the way the miners lived. Yet the war was in folks' minds, both Confederate and Union sympathizers. Confederates didn't say much, as Union men did, for Union men were in the majority. Sam Clemens, former Confederate soldier of a few weeks' service, now believed in preservation of the union, and was antislavery in his views. Still, he thought it best not to express such controversial opinions in the public print. Sam had made up his mind not to become a target for anyone's bullets.

When the city editor of the *Enterprise* wrote a factual story he signed his own name to it, but when he wrote a funny one he often put on it the name of "Mark Twain." The old river pilot Sellers was dead and Sam felt that, somehow, his use of the name would be a private tribute. For a while he was a double personality in print, but as people knew him better, he shifted over to the new name, and before long he was being called Mark by everybody. He liked the sound of the old leadsman's cry of the Mississippi, and it seemed to suit him. Under the name Mark Twain he brought smiles, chuckles, and guffaws to the faces of miners. When news got a bit dull — no hanging, duel, arrival of an immigrant wagon train, or even a school picnic — then Mark Twain felt that it was his plain duty to stir things up somewhat.

On one occasion he thought that the latest excitement, a great to-do over some so-called petrified bones found in the diggings, was more than a little silly. He would show up this nonsense. He would write a hoax. And why not kill two birds with one petrified bone? There was a fellow whom he disliked, a coroner living in Humboldt. Mark thought that he would just "touch him up and make him ridiculous, and thus combine pleasure with business."

The story was a sensation! Mark Twain thought that any fool would realize that the "facts" in his account of the finding of the petrified man were all impossibilities. He had told of an inquest held by the coroner in Humboldt on a man who had been turned to stone three hundred years ago. He said that the coroner's verdict was that the death had occurred from "protracted exposure." But it was in the description of the position of the petrified man that the reader must surely be enlightened. The stone man was sitting with his hands thumbing his nose! Nobody took time to think about it, and news of this remarkable discovery went out by telegraph all over the world. As newspapers came in from all over, one after the other, in large numbers, containing stories about the Western wonder in Nevada, Mark sent them all on to his enemy in Humboldt. The coroner piled the papers in mountainous stacks behind his house, and was ready to shoot his friends, when they came in to ask innocently, "Say, can you tell me where I can get hold of a paper with the Petrified Man in it?" Mark ended his account of the hoax with the remark that he "couldn't have gotten more real comfort out of that coroner without killing him."

Another story by Mark Twain enlivened a dull moment in the city a little later. The writer claimed that he was only trying to show up the crooked mining companies, those that cheated the investor by declaring a "crooked," or false, dividend. Mark wrote his story about a poor miner who was ruined by such a company, and as a result murdered his wife and baby in an especially gruesome manner and then killed himself. It was called "The Empire City Massacre" and it was as full of impossibilities as a horse thief was full of holes when caught with the goods. But it was taken as sober truth and was the talk of the town. Bearded miners turned pale and lost their appetites when reading it. Its fame spread out beyond Nevada and it made a sensation wherever it was read. Mark had written into it so many gory details that readers never got beyond them and failed utterly to see the moral.

Sam Clemens was young, still in his twenties. He was cocksure, his tongue was sometimes sharp, and his pen sharper. He made enemies, but he made far more friends. He was a rolling stone in those days, and by 1863 he was getting restless again.

He had been in Virginia City for two years. Again, as in the early days in Hannibal, Sam was left in charge of the paper while the editor went on a trip. This was in April, 1864.

An editorial that was far from complimentary was published about a rival editor named Laird. Although a law had recently been passed against dueling, Laird ignored the fact and sent Mark a challenge. Mark couldn't shoot worth a cent, and he only hoped that Laird couldn't do any better. He took his friend, Steve Gillis, and went unhappily to the spot chosen for the duel. He felt that he needed some practice. A barn was handy, but Mark inspected it carefully after shooting at it, and couldn't find a scratch. To add to his uneasiness, he could hear practice shots in the next gulch. A tiny bird flew by, and Steve drew his revolver and shot it down. As Mark picked up the bird to look at it, Laird and his second came out of the gulch. Quick as a flash, Steve spoke up and announced that Clemens had shot the sparrow. Mr. Laird's jaw dropped. He stammered out an apology and his second helped him shakily home.

The following morning news circulated that Mark Twain

had fought a duel in direct violation of the new law. Sam and Steve took the next stagecoach for San Francisco.

In the stage, rolling along to California, he was coming into another phase of his adventurous life. Cigar in mouth, boots propped once again on a pile of mail sacks, Sam Clemens, now known in the West as Mark Twain, came bounding down the High Sierras. From the coach windows he saw a land fifteen years older than it was when the discovery of glittering particles in a creek suddenly turned a country of Spanish ranches into the fantastic Gold Rush of 1849.

Now he could see towns, once roaring with mining fever, becoming ghostly collections of wooden shacks, crumbling silently to ruin with the end of the big times. And he saw others, steadily growing into permanent centers for farms and business. San Francisco was building in giant steps up its steep hillsides overlooking the blue bay where vessels rode at anchor. Gold Rush over, Mark saw a rich land — a hardy, tough, flourishing place.

He soon found a job as reporter on the *Morning Call*. This was not the best newspaper in town, and restless Mark Twain found the work dull as well as underpaid. After a few months he was fired from the *Morning Call*, and decided to go mining for gold with a brother of Steve Gillis, and his friend Dick Stoker.

The three lived in Jackass Gulch, and wandered around every day searching for "pockets" of gold. A "pocket" was hard to come by, but a lucky find could yield a lot of gold without much effort. Mark did not find enough gold to pay for his keep — but he found a few rich "pockets" of tales and stories. Jim Gillis was a natural storyteller, and one of the best. It was from Jim that Sam first heard the story of "The Celebrated Jumping Frog of Calaveras County."

After a few months Sam returned to the city by the Golden Gate and went to work for a literary paper, *The Golden Era.* This was in 1866. Bret Harte, writer of "The Luck of Roaring Camp" and other mining stories that made him famous, was a fellow member of the staff. Stories signed by Mark Twain also went to the *Enterprise* in Virginia City. But Sam Clemens was restless again. He persuaded the Sacramento *Union* to send him to the Sandwich Islands, as Hawaii was then known, to write a series of stories on the sugar plantations. While there he made a well-publicized "scoop" for his paper, with a news story of an important shipwreck.

When Sam stepped onto the dock at San Francisco again he found his writing and his name, Mark Twain, famous throughout the West. The popular humorist and lecturer Artemus Ward met Mark in San Francisco and heard him tell the story of the jumping frog. He urged Mark to publish the tale, and also to give lectures.

Well, thought Mark, why not? This was a new idea, to go on the lecture platform, but he was sure that he could do better than some lecturers he had heard. When he mentioned the idea to friends, the owner of a theater in the city offered to put him on.

Posters read: "Doors open at 7 o'clock. The trouble will start at 8." Would anybody come to hear him? Mark nearly died of nervousness wondering, but when he arrived at the door he found the hall so packed that there wasn't any standing room left. He had cold hands, and feet that seemed numb, and yet he walked onto the platform as easily as if he were strolling into a friend's home. In his drawling, serious voice, in the way his mother had always called "Sammy's slow talk," Mark Twain began to speak. He had a habit of walking about as he talked, or leaning against a stand or table, fiddling with his watch chain, and lighting, very deliberately, his rank black cigar. He told a funny story — a story that often had a sly comment on society, customs or events — and he told it with a pause of just the right split-second length, near the end, followed by a remark so pointed, incongruous, or just plain ridiculous, that his audience broke up into gales of delighted laughter. He could poke fun at himself and at everybody else.

He told the story of the champion frog that lost the jumping contest because he had been filled with buckshot, and of the stranger who owned the winning frog. The stranger ambled away, winnings in his pocket, remarking, "Well, *I* don't see no p'ints about that frog that's better'n any other frog!"

It wasn't long before people could be heard all over San Francisco, breaking into laughter, saying, "Well, *I* don't see no p'ints about that frog that's better'n any other frog."

A man who went west in the early days had to rough it. He might be scared by encounters with Indians, highwaymen, or mountain lions, but if he wasn't ready to cope with a crisis at any moment he had to go under or return to the east. When Horace Greeley, of the New York Tribune, went west on a trip, he discovered that his frightening experiences had left no bad aftereffects. But the story told about this distinguished editor by a lecturer who called himself Mark Twain made Horace Greeley the laughing stock of the nation.

Sam Clemens' ventures into prospecting and gold mining produced one unfortunate result after another. In Virginia City, Nevada, he discovered that he had special talents as a newspaper writer. When the intermittent street shootings and wild brawls did not provide enough lively copy for him, he used his imagination to "stir up his readers a little." These stories were reprinted by other papers all across the country, and often taken for the truth. Yet they were no stranger than some of his real adventures, such as the fight in a tavern in which the owner's wife subdued a ferocious fighting man with a pair of scissors.

Mark Twain never forgot his western friends and the many stories that he heard them tell. When he put them into his writings he added his own humor and understanding and they came out such tales as only this writer could produce. The new "lingo" of the west, with its mixture of every kind of talk, from Indian to English, to Chinese, brought some strange incidents into print. And the conversation of such different men as parsons and miners was uproariously funny. No one who ever read Mark Twain's description of the conversation about Buck Fanshaw's funeral could remember it without l̶ ̶ ̶hter.

Mark Twain on the platform was as humorous as he was in print. One of his most famous anecdotes was the story of Jim Blaine and his grandfather's old ram. Listeners in the lecture hall, or readers of *Roughing It*, might be waiting anxiously to find out all about that ram, but what they got in the story was not merely unpredictable. It was unforgettable.

Among Mark Twain's best friends there were many cats, both real and imaginary. One of his favorite stories of the California Gold Fields, when he lived on Jackass Hill, was about a cat named Tom Quartz. What Tom knew about mining was surprising. And how he learned it was startling.

5

Young Man, Go East!

THE SMALL MINING HALL rocked with howls of glee, stamping boots, and clapping hands. Tallow candles sputtered on the rickety stage in front of torn red curtains, and behind the bearded audience oil lanterns swayed from the rafters. Mark Twain was on his first lecturing "raid" in California, and every hall, whether it was the Opera House or a place such as this one, echoed with a storm of appreciation when he stepped down. Mark bowed and shook hands with all who came to greet him. A little old man at the end of the line looked at him, shifted his tobacco plug to the other cheek, spit accurately into a brass spittoon some distance away, and said, "Be them your natural tones of eloquence?"

Mark carried his "raid" back to his old hangouts in Nevada, where his reception was wild and enthusiastic. When he was ready to leave for California again, more lectures were demanded, but Mark refused. So some old cronies of Virginia City made a secret plan to disguise themselves and rob Sam on the Divide between Gold Hill and Virginia City, where more than one real holdup had taken place. They thought that Mark would give more lectures to fill his purse again, and that they could then return his money.

Mark didn't appear excited or frightened as bandits with black masks and disguised voices demanded his valuables. When he lowered his hands to get his money out, the robbers ordered his hands up again.

"Well," drawled Mark, "how do you expect me to give you my valuables with my hands up in the sky? My treasures don't lie — in heaven."

It was a cold night. By the time that Mark and his manager had reached the next town they had caught colds. That night somebody gave away the joke and Mark felt in no condition to be amused. It took Joe Goodman several hours to talk him out of having the others arrested. Mark still refused to give more lectures in Nevada. Yet when the stage left next morning he put his head out of the window and called, "Good-by friends — and thieves. I bear you no malice."

In San Francisco Mark took a ship for New York, sailed to Panama, crossed the jungle of the isthmus on mule back, and boarded another ship in the Gulf of Mexico. Before they were many days out, a seaman came down with cholera, and six on board had died by the time they reached port. It was a long and terrible voyage, but Mark managed to escape the cholera. In New York he set about arranging to have his "Jumping Frog" and some other short sketches published in a book, and when his business was settled he took a train for home.

It had been more than five years since Sam had left his mother and sister and the great river of his youth. Jane and Pamela laughed and cried at sight of him and found him the same Sam — solemn-faced, slow-talking, with a twinkle in the eye. Jane found it hard to believe that her black sheep was famous in the West, especially when he teased her in the old way. He went back to Hannibal, gave a lecture in the town hall, and swapped yarns with his friends again.

Mark soon decided that he must see the world beyond his own

national boundaries. When he read an announcement of the sailing of a pleasure excursion to foreign lands, the first "tour" in history, he knew that he had to be on board. Although this five-month voyage to Europe and the Holy Land was called a "picnic on the seas" it was not to be taken lightly, for it was planned for religious travelers. Mark telegraphed the *Alta California,* a newspaper, described the tour, and asked to be sent as special correspondent. To his astonishment the reply came quickly. The newspaper would pay his way and he would send them letters for publication at a rate of twenty dollars per letter. Back in New York Mark persuaded the *Tribune* to take some letters also. He booked passage on the *Quaker City* steamship and was surprised and delighted to learn that the passengers listed as celebrated were General Sherman, the Reverend Mr. Henry Ward Beecher — and Mark Twain! The first two withdrew from the voyage, but Mark Twain was on the *Quaker City* when it sailed in June.

It was because he was on board that this "picnic on the seas" was not forgotten but was made immortal between the covers of a book, *The Innocents Abroad* — the most popular travel book ever written.

A month before he sailed, Mark Twain's *The Celebrated Jumping Frog of Calaveras County, and Other Sketches* was published. Despite the excitement of holding in his hand his first book, small volume though it was, Mark was more concerned with a lecture that he was scheduled to give at Cooper Union, the largest hall in New York City. He was terrified at the thought that the hall might be empty when he came out on the stage, and so he gave away a large number of tickets to schoolteachers. When he arrived at the hall and found the whole street jammed with an overflow crowd his spirits rose like a kite in a high wind — and the applause and laughter greeting the conclusion of his program almost deafened him. He made very little money because of the free tickets, but he was always grateful to the schoolteachers for coming in such numbers.

On board the *Quaker City* Mark found himself in a group that was rather more pious than he was used to. Yet he was always fond of preachers, if they weren't too pompus, and he soon had a group of the more congenial spirits around him. His roommate was the lively Dan Slote. The ship's doctor was a boon companion too, and so was Jack Van Nostrand. It was these three, with Mark himself, who made life such a burden to the Italian guides, as Mark Twain told later in *The Innocents Abroad*. When a guide showed them the logbook of the great Columbus, waiting with eager expectancy to hear their cries of astonishment, one of the four would ask, after a long, blank silence, "Columbus? Who was he? Is he dead?"

There were others on board who made the voyage pleasant

for Mark. One of them was an older woman, known to them as Mother Fairbanks, wife of a newspaper editor. She read Mark's writings with appreciation and also with a critical eye, and gave him much good advice.

Five months of sailing, through fair and stormy weather, to France, Italy, Greece, Egypt, and the Holy Land! Mark learned to avoid the bores whenever possible. One such passenger was a well-to-do farmer from Long Island who had literary pretensions and who inflicted his verses on everybody. He had a collection of these verses printed and ready to hand out, and in addition wrote new verses daily. One of these Mark remembered as "An Ode to a Rooster in the Waist of the Ship." For his part Mark also wrote every day, carrying his paper and pencils around with him. During these months he sent back to his newspapers a total of about 250,000 words, telling Americans all about the cities, canals, castles, and other wonders of the Old World, as well as about the Old Masters, whose paintings he refused to admire. When Mark Twain wrote he laughed at everybody, including himself. He made fun of pretense, of sham and of hypocrisy. Americans chuckled and rejoiced when they read of this innocent abroad, for never before had a book of travel done anything but solemnly attempt to educate and uplift them.

A young man of eighteen named Charles Langdon was in the party on shipboard. Visiting his stateroom while the vessel rocked at anchor in the Bay of Smyrna, Mark saw a delicate portrait of a young girl, painted on ivory. This was the face of Charley's sister, Olivia. Mark could not take his eyes from her serious, sensitive features, and he set himself to think up many and varied excuses to go to Charley's room to look at it over and over.

Finally the five-month-long "picnic at sea" was over, and Mark took stock of his prospects. What to do now? He accepted an offer to serve in Washington as secretary to a senator from the West. He wasn't a secretary long, for his comments on life in the capital, and on congressmen in particular, along with a refusal to take his routine job seriously, got him fired after a few months.

At Christmas Mark was invited to visit Dan Slote in New York City, and join a reunion of a few of the "fellow innocents." This was followed by a visit to Charley Langdon at the St. Nicholas Hotel, where Mark was introduced to Mr. and Mrs. Jervis Langdon and to Miss Olivia Langdon. Sam Clemens, a man of thirty-one, felt like an awkward youth again as he took the hand of Olivia Langdon, and saw before him a young girl, sweet and shy, as lovely as the delicate ivory miniature.

The Langdons were going to a reading to be given by Charles Dickens, and Mark went with them. Although he heard Dickens read from *David Copperfield,* and although his eyes were fixed on the dramatic figure of the great author in his black velvet suit with the scarlet flower in his buttonhole, Mark was conscious only of the fact that he, Samuel Clemens, sat beside Olivia Langdon.

Mark eagerly accepted an invitation to visit the Langdon home in Elmira, New York, without realizing that more than a year would pass before he could go there. He had been thinking of making a book of his letters from the *Quaker City* voyage, and was happy to receive a request for such a book from an editor in a Hartford, Connecticut, publishing house. To do it, Mark had to go to California, persuade the newspaper editors to let him have the letters that he had written, edit them, add more writing, and make a unified book of the whole.

After he had finished his book Mark went on a lecturing tour that covered the country. He soon became a favorite lecturer, and his evenings were so popular that not even the most famous actress of the day could compete with him in the same town on the same evening. When the book was in proof Mark went to Hartford, read his proof, and then took a train for Elmira.

There he was greeted with pleasure by Mr. and Mrs. Langdon and by a shy, smiling Olivia. Charley was glad to see him also, until he suspected that Mark was courting his sister, and then he began to look on his friend with grave doubts.

Livy just didn't know what to make of this suitor, who was hanging around her "like Grant around Richmond." She laughed at him, and was sometimes shocked by him. She knew him to be gentle and kind, with a ready sympathy for anyone, or any animal, in trouble. He was rough and Western, smoked strong, cheap cigars all day, and even at night, when wisps of rank smoke curled out under his door and gave him away. He was brilliant, and quaint, and very funny when he wanted to be. He looked older than he was, and yet he seemed much younger in spirit. Livy took to calling him by a special name — "Youth." She turned down his proposal of marriage over and over, and then she found that she could not live without him, and accepted him.

Mr. Langdon thought that it was his fatherly duty to ask the suitor for "credentials." Mark gave him the names of several highly respectable pillars of society in the West, but when the answers arrived they all said that Samuel Clemens was a man of talent who would make the worst possible hus-

band. Mr. Langdon looked at Mark, who dejectedly fingered his cold cigar.

"Samuel, you seem to have no friends. But — well — you do have one."

Mark's head came slowly up. "Who?" he asked.

"I am your friend. I believe in you. I know you better than they do." With that he gave his consent and the engagement was announced the next day.

On publication *The Innocents Abroad* made a sensation. William Dean Howells, editor of *The Atlantic Monthly,* acclaimed it as a great travel book, and it became the most popular book of humor ever published up to that time. Mark Twain was famous in the East and West. His sayings were quoted and reprinted in newspapers everywhere. The book became as well liked in England as in America, and it was in England, and not in New England, that Mark Twain was hailed as a great literary man. The New England authors, such as Longfellow, Lowell, Holmes, and Emerson thought it "quaint" and "amusing" and they read it with pleasure, but the idea that Mark Twain might be a literary figure did not seem to be considered until many years later.

As a matter of fact even Mark did not consider himself a literary man at this time. He thought of himself as a journalist, and expected to make his living as one. Looking around for a post on a newspaper he located one with the Buffalo *Express,* and bought a part interest in the paper. Buffalo wasn't far from Elmira, and he and Livy could see the Langdons often if they lived there.

The minister who married Olivia Langdon and Samuel Clemens was Joseph Twitchell of Hartford. Mark had met Joe there while the proofs of *Innocents Abroad* were being read, and these two men had taken a great liking to each other. He and his wife accompanied the whole wedding party to Buffalo to escort the bride and groom to their new home, and to see Mark's astonishment when he was taken to a house given them, furniture and all, by Mr. Langdon.

Mark and Livy settled down to their new life together, looked after by their cook and the coachman, young Patrick McAleer, who became a lifelong friend as well. Mark thought from time to time of a free-lance writing career, but had his doubts about it. He was afraid that he could not make a steady living that way. On the Buffalo *Express* he was both editor and writer of a column, and he worked hard at his new job.

When he returned home from his office of an evening, he ate a good dinner with his bride. Then he rose from the table to march around and around, in that odd ambling walk of his, and talk of everything that had happened during the day. He also teased Livy, catching her unawares, until she dropped her fork on her plate to laugh and protest, as Jane Clemens had done. But she did not say, "Sam! You, SAM!" Instead she said, "Youth! Oh, Youth!"

A PREVIEW OF

Innocents Abroad

or THE NEW PILGRIMS' PROGRESS

Mark Twain had laughed at "greenhorns" from the east who knew nothing of western ways. Now he was a "greenhorn" himself on the steamship Quaker City bound for Europe and the Holy Land. In the newspaper stories that he wrote on board ship he made fun of his own ignorance as well as that of his friends. These travelers were truly innocents abroad. And no ridiculous scene escaped the eye and pen of Mark Twain. Riding horses, mules and donkeys was an old story to him. But riding a donkey on a Portuguese island in the Azores was something new! And the way that he wrote about it was new to American readers when the book about his voyage was published.

There were wonderful experiences ahead for those sailing on the first voyage arranged as a pleasure cruise. Paris in mid-nineteenth century was breathtaking. Even Mark Twain would not have missed the sight of Emperor Napoleon III riding through the Bois de Boulogne park with the Sultan of Turkey by his side. Yet Mark Twain's irreverent humor and strong sense of democracy kept him from being fooled by fancy clothes or royal titles.

Mark Twain called his fellow travelers "the Pilgrims" and himself, along with several of his buddies, "the Unholy Pilgrims." These unholies had special talents for amusing themselves at the expense of their guides. Even when they were gazing in awe at ancient relics they could not resist the temptation to demoralize the guides. The sight of a mummy in Rome was too good a chance to pass up. And when Mark Twain and his friends suspected that the sights shown to them were not genuine—then guides beware!

The passengers felt that their voyage would not be a success without a visit to the ancient Greek Parthenon. Just as they were ready to disembark, quarantine officers came aboard to forbid them to leave ship for eleven days. Since the vessel could not remain in one port that long the "Pilgrims" were disappointed. The "Unholy Pilgrims" made their own plans. Late that night Mark and three friends slipped ashore secretly in a small boat, and then sneaked on foot up to the Acropolis hill to view the ruins, the columns and the statues. They got there without trouble, but the return to their boat stirred up the countryside. Their leader was, fortunately, a westerner named Clemens who had dodged pursuers before. What were Greek policemen compared to Indians, bandits or enraged miners?

To a man who had lived on the hot plains and in the high mountains of the American west in its wild days, riding under an umbrella was absurd. Even worse, these tourists wore green spectacles. Mark Twain refused to do either. He wrote—"Here, you feel all the time just as if you were living about the year 1200 before Christ . . . The scenery of the Bible is about you—the customs . . . the same people . . . and behold . . . comes this fantastic mob of green-spectacled Yanks, with their flapping elbows and bobbing umbrellas!" He thought that it would be bad enough to have a sunstroke—but worse to appear so ridiculous. Yet, despite his foolery, a visit to the Holy Land was a sincerely deep and moving experience for this young writer from the frontiers of America.

6

"As Mark Twain Says —"

THE FIRST FIFTEEN MONTHS of their marriage were filled with lights and shadows for Mr. and Mrs. Samuel Clemens. They were happy together, and Mark worked hard both on his newspaper and on magazine articles. Then Jervis Langdon became ill, and Mark and Livy went to Elmira to help take care of him. When he died they returned in sorrow to Buffalo, accompanied by a girlhood friend of Livy's, who was to keep her company for a while. This friend was taken ill with typhoid fever, and after a period of day and night nursing by the Clemenses, died in their home. A few months later their first child, Langdon, was born prematurely, and for some months both baby and mother were ill.

Mark was beginning to realize that he no longer enjoyed newspaper work. He was making a good income as a free-lance writer and Livy had inherited money from her father. Their Buffalo home held sad memories for them, and Buffalo itself was a business town. Mark was attracted by Hartford, with its literary group. He and Livy decided to move to Hartford, and Mark came to a decision to devote his entire time to free-lance literary work.

In the autumn of 1871 friendly neighbors of the Nook Farm section of the Connecticut city gathered to welcome the newcomers. These neighbors included Charles Dudley Warner, novelist, and Harriet Beecher Stowe, whose *Uncle Tom's Cabin* was world-famous. Mark's best friend, the minister, Joe Twitchell, and his wife were there also to greet a Mark Twain, thin and weary but with spirits rising high at sight of this new home. Mrs. Clemens was pale and ill, showing the long strain. A nurse carrying tiny Langdon, not yet a year old, was followed into the house by brisk, cheerful Patrick McAleer.

In March of the following spring they returned to Elmira for a time. Here their second child was born. She was named Susan for her aunt, Livy's sister, Susy Crane. As soon as summer came the Clemens family joined Mr. and Mrs. Theodore Crane at Quarry Farm, near Elmira.

Mark loved the quiet, happy life on the farm, and he wrote best there. His new book, *Roughing It,* was almost as popular as *The Innocents Abroad,* and money came in well. Yet sorrow would not give up its hold on their lives, for that summer little Langdon died of diphtheria. Mark blamed himself for the tragic loss of his firstborn, because he had let the covers slip off while taking the baby driving. This blame, which he assumed with every family trouble and never with any real cause, came from the sensitive conscience of a man who as a boy had expected a lightning bolt to strike him down for disobedience when he played hooky from school. It was the sorrowful echo of the grief, and the sense of being personally responsible, that Sam Clemens had felt when his brother Henry had died long ago in the wreck of a Mississippi steamboat.

During these first years of marriage, when Mark's life was so filled with both joy and grief, his professional reputation grew to enormous proportions. He was better known than any other living American, and his works were trans-

lated into many foreign languages. A letter addressed simply to "Mark Twain" reached him without delay. A mandarin in China, a scholar in Persia, a workman in Ireland, a cowboy on the plains of Texas — if asked would reply, "Of course I read Mark Twain's books." Yet the literary "greats" of New England, the center of American culture, still refused to call him anything but a clever, funny man. Bret Harte, who was also a Westerner, was accepted as an important author by the Eastern critics, but not Mark Twain. Mark shrugged off this judgment, yet he could not forget it.

Despite this, Mark, whose moods could go down very low, was a happy man. His sense of humor always brought him up again, and his life with Livy and healthy, rosy Susy was good. He could not help looking on life with a twinkle in his gray eyes, a funny comment on his slow tongue — and a joke waiting to be played on somebody. It was Livy who was teased most often, and who never knew what was coming next — to make her laugh and cry out "Oh, Youth!"

The Clemenses bought a piece of land along a stream not far from the rented house that they lived in, and built a home designed by a popular architect. He constructed it on what he called the "violet plan." It had a remarkable array of large rooms, turrets, porches, balconies, and a conservatory filled with plants in the fanciful Victorian style. Mark enjoyed a big, rambling house, many servants, carriages, and guests coming and going every day. He was wildly extravagant in his expenditure of money for his home. He liked parties with charades and impromptu plays — directed by him — and a vast ocean of good conversation, in which he was always the central attraction. The guests burst into laughter when Mark ambled in, as a steamboat character or a miner from Jackass Gulch. Most of all, Mark liked to hear Livy murmur disap-

provingly, even as she laughed, "Youth!"

Distinguished visitors came to see Mark Twain. Matthew Arnold, an English writer, found it hard to leave when he visited the Clemens home. He asked a friend, "Is he never serious?" The friend replied, "Mr. Arnold, Mark Twain is the most serious man in the world." For all his fun, Mark Twain had a vast, deep feeling for humanity, a hatred for injustice and cruelty, and an urge, which he seldom denied, to show up sham.

Mark also had a happy enthusiasm for almost everything. He and his preacher friend Joe Twitchell decided to learn to ride a new contraption called the bicycle. This was a vehicle with an enormous wheel in front, a small wheel behind, and no brakes. Just to learn balance was a feat of no mean char-

111

acter. They hired a young German to teach them to ride. He escorted them out, and up and down the street, very early in the morning before the neighbors were up. Joe Twitchell got the hang of it pretty well, but Mark was slower. After the first lesson the teacher said, "Mr. Clemens, you can fall off a bicycle more ways than the man who invented it!" Mark always claimed that he himself was the one who thought up all of the new profanity connected with bicycles that has since come into use. They learned to ride, but never enjoyed it and soon gave it up.

Mark was popular with the literary set of Hartford and Boston, even though their respect for his ability as an author was not as high at it should have been. Perhaps it was because he knew this that Mark was so pleased when he was asked to give the address at a dinner to be held in Boston in honor of John Greenleaf Whittier.

Mark decided that he must do something really special and humorous. Somehow he never was able to realize fully, until it was too late, that a joke or a hoax could be as dangerous as a bombshell. When he got such an idea he lost touch with his normal consideration for others. And he made the mistake of getting such an idea for his speech to be delivered at the formal, literary dinner given by the staff of *The Atlantic Monthly* magazine. The joke was a story making fun of the works of Longfellow, Emerson, and Holmes, all of whom were guests at the banquet. Mark told the tale of three drunken miners who pretended to be these three distinguished authors, and he even gave ridiculous parodies of their poems. It was funny — but not to the company who heard it. Nobody laughed. In a deep, disapproving silence the joke fell flat. Next day Mark was so overcome with remorse and shame at his tactlessness that he apologized, and, although the others forgave him at once, he never forgave himself. The lampooned authors were not angry, but Mark added this incident to the load on his sensitive conscience.

He depended on Livy to keep him straight on deportment, and she tried to do it. They were a happy couple, although so different. Yet Livy never succeeded in toning down her "Youth" very much. She was always disturbed by his fantastic swearing, the result of years on the river and in the West. Mark respected her feelings, and tried to do his swearing away from the house somewhere.

One Sunday morning when he thought Livy asleep in the next room and did not know that the door was ajar, Mark found a button off his shirt. He swore softly, and threw the shirt out of the window. The second shirt had a button off. He swore louder, adding more picturesque details — and hurled that one into the shrubbery. A third shirt was without a button. He let go, in his old ripsnorting mining language.

When he stopped he heard a slight sound. Creeping into the bedroom he saw Livy, eyes indignant, and heard her gentle voice repeating the last lurid, lightning-and-thunder remark, hoping to shame him. He burst out laughing, saying, "Livy, you've got the words — but you don't know the tune."

When Susy was a lively two-year-old a little sister arrived in the Clemens family. The baby was named Clara, but as she grew older her father reduced the name of "Baby" to "Bay." He often called Susy "Modoc," saying that he really believed that she belonged to the Modoc tribe of Indians. Mark frequently sat in the library with "Modoc" and "Bay," one on each knee, making up a story as he talked. Their favorite tales always began with the picture on the wall of a girl called Emaline, and traveled along a row of bric-a-brac to a picture of a cat. Although the audience demanded that the story take up these objects in this order, somehow the tales always came out differently, and the imagination of Mark Twain never let his small listeners lose interest.

Mark loved cats all of his life. He was willing to be friendly with a dog, and he even grew fond of a dog named Bones at Quarry Farm, but he respected cats, and liked their independence. He always had cats around him. He gave them such names as Blatherskite, Sour Mash, Sin, Satan, Stray Kit, and Fräulein. Susy said once, "The difference between Papa and Mama is that Mama loves morals and Papa loves cats."

Mark enjoyed his billiard room on the top floor. There he drew visitors into his game, talked and joked, and also did his writing. Down the stairway to Livy and the children drifted clouds of smoke, the click of billiard balls, and laughter. The visitor might be Rudyard Kipling, Robert Louis Stevenson — or one of Mark's old companions of his wild days in the West.

Nearly every summer the family returned to Quarry Farm, and the two children, now joined by a third sister, whose name was Jean, ran in the fields and played in the farmyard. Mrs. Theodore Crane had had a small eight-sided study built for Mark on the hillside some distance from the house, and he seemed to work better there than elsewhere. The study had windows all around and a tiny fireplace for chilly days. Here Mark Twain had written *Roughing It,* and here later were to be written *The Adventures of Tom Sawyer, The Adventures of Huckleberry Finn, A Connecticut Yankee in King Arthur's Court,* and *The Prince and the Pauper.* Most of his books were not finished at once, and he worked on them also in Hartford. Often Mark Twain would allow a manuscript to lie unfinished for several years, and would then go at it again and complete the book, in the study that looked like a ship's pilothouse.

His daily pattern at Quarry Farm became fixed. He rose rather late and had a big breakfast, then went to the little study for four or five hours. When he came down again in late afternoon he went with the children to ride home on the hay wagon, played games with them, and took small Jean to see her friends the cows. Sometimes he stretched out under the trees in a hammock beside another hammock containing his brother-in-law, and they would read aloud until supper, as Livy and her sister, Sue Crane, rocked on the veranda.

In the evening, with the children asleep upstairs, they sat on the porch and talked lazily, watching the moonlight gild the meadows and hills. Sometimes the Negro cook, old Auntie Cord, came around with George, the butler, to sit on the steps and talk about her slave days in the South. When Mark wrote of the days before the war he used the real language common to that period, yet he had a deep respect and liking for the

Negro race, a high regard that appeared in everything that he wrote about them. One of his most moving and serious magazine stories was the true account of Auntie Cord's separation from her children when they were taken from her to be sold to another master.

Often Mark gathered up his sheets of paper, covered with his large handwriting, and brought them down for a critical reading by his wife. When Livy thought a word or sentence should go, he struck it out, though not without argument.

When his daughters grew older they joined the critical group. Sometimes Mark purposely put in things that he knew would not pass Livy's censorious eye. He chuckled as the children begged to have these "horrible" things left in and Livy ruthlessly struck them out. One of his stories most enjoyed by Livy and the children was a tale called *The Prince and the Pauper*. They laughed and cried with the little beggar boy and the young prince, mistaken for each other in England at the time of Henry the Eighth.

Susy Clemens was a slender girl of thirteen when she began to write a diary that was meant to be a biography of her famous father. She wrote, "We are a very happy family. It is Papa that I am writing about, and I shall have no trouble in not knowing what to say about him, for he is a very striking character." These were years when honors from the distinguished, the rich, and the powerful of the earth came thick and fast to Mark Twain. Yet he felt that no honor could ever come up to that of having been chosen to be the subject of Susy's little biography.

The PRINCE
and the Pauper

Mark Twain was always interested in the idea of twins who looked exactly alike. What would a boy prince do if he became a beggar in the slums of London, and what would happen to him? Could a street waif wear the clothing and power of a prince and get away with it?

The little prince longed for freedom from court life, with its rules and duties for every hour of the day. How wonderful he thought it would be to get out alone into the great city where no one cared who you were or what you might do! A beggar's life must be a long adventure. Could he persuade this street boy to take on the dull life of a future king?

The young prince, unprotected and alone, walked into the worst quarter of London, with its thieves and assassins. He was like a lamb going into a den of wild beasts. He could not have survived long had he not found a friend called Miles to protect him.

The future king was learning a great deal about his kingdom and the way in which his subjects really lived. He joined the huge mob of street beggars, some real and some fake, and was saved from persecution and danger many times by the courage and skill of his protector.

There came a terrible time when not even Miles could keep the prince from learning at first hand what life was like in prison. The confinement of a palace was not so bad after all, compared with the barred windows and stone walls of a dungeon. And tutors, attendants and courtiers made far better companions for a young prince than brutal jailers and dangerous prisoners. If he ever got out again the prince would not forget these things.

What kind of life was the false prince leading? And how was he handling the responsibilities of his high place? The lost prince wondered about these things as he tried to figure out how to get back to his palace. His need to return became more urgent when the old king died, and Coronation Day drew near. Who would be crowned king? The prince or the pauper?

7

Around the World on a "Raid"

It was in 1879 that Mark Twain met General Grant for the second time. The general had stirred his admiration as no other great military man had ever done. Their first meeting had taken place twelve years before, when Mark was a journalist and secretary in Washington, and had asked the war hero for an interview. For once the intrepid Mark, known even then as the "Wild Humorist of the Pacific Slope," had been stricken silent, while the general, a man of few words, stared solemnly at him.

Then Mark said slowly, "General, I seem to be a little embarrassed. Are you?"

And now the man who had been a Confederate soldier, chased through the woods of Missouri for several weeks, was invited to speak at a national reunion of the Union Armies, gathered to honor General Grant. Mark had always claimed that it was the great Grant himself who was right on his heels during those two weeks in Missouri, although he couldn't prove it! He traveled to Chicago, and was introduced to the guest of honor by the mayor of Chicago: "General, let me present Mr. Clemens, a man almost as great as yourself." With a little twinkle in his eye the general replied, "Mr. Clemens, *I* am not embarrassed. Are *you?*"

During those years when Mark lived in Hartford in a

fashion that satisfied his love of company, he still had the urge to travel. He went on lecture tours that took him across the country, and he was always ready to travel for pleasure too. The Clemens family visited England, Scotland, and most of Europe, where Mark Twain received a royal welcome everywhere. After they returned to Hartford they took a trip to Keokuk to see Orion, his wife, and Jane Clemens. Traveling on a riverboat once more, Mark heard the big bells ring for soundings, and the old cries — "Mark twain! Mark twain!" Susy came running to him, out of breath, calling out, "Papa, I've hunted everywhere for you. Why don't you answer when they call you?"

That summer Susy stopped writing her biography. She ended it with a sentence half finished, and her father did not know why, except that she was more interested now in her studies and her music. Susy was a talented child, sensitive, creative like her father, and with a feeling for words. Yet she was also nervous and high-strung, and often ill. She did not have her father's ability to relax, or her mother's quiet spirit. Mark and Livy worried about her health and her father tried to find all sorts of new health cures, even as his own personal problems grew.

His mail, for instance, was becoming an increasing burden to Mark. During a lecture trip with George W. Cable, he complained of this, and especially of the autograph hunters. This gave Cable an idea. He wrote to a number of Mark's friends, asking each one to request an autograph, timing it so that these letters all arrived on April Fool's Day. Mark suspected nothing. Then as he opened letter after letter the twinkle came into his eyes and he began to laugh. The letters asked for all sorts of autographs, put in requests for him to copy a long hymn, demanded autographs for books that he had not written; they came from the distinguished actor, Henry Irving, from Joe Twitchell, and his other close friends, from famous writers, editors, artists, politicians, and ministers, including Henry Ward Beecher. One hundred and fifty friends took delight in playing a joke on Mark Twain — and thereby proving their friendship also.

Mark did a lot of letter writing himself. When he received a notice from England saying that there was a rumor that he was going to buy a home in that country, and that he would therefore have to pay a tax, he wrote a reply that was printed in *Harper's Magazine.* In this letter he said that he had never met Queen Victoria, but that he had met her son, Prince Edward. He met him while the Prince was leading a procession in Oxford Street, and the Prince would remember him because he was on top of a bus and was wearing his new overcoat with flap pockets. This letter was reprinted widely, not only in America but in England as well.

Although Mark Twain had not bought an estate in England, he was closely involved with that country, for he was writing a book called *A Connecticut Yankee in King Arthur's Court.* This was the tale of an American carried back in time to the court of King Arthur. As a boy Sam Clemens had loved the stories of chivalry and knighthood. This interest had continued through the years. He first read that fine book, Mallory's *Morte d'Arthur,* while on a lecture tour with Cable, and since then had enjoyed other tales written of the period. Mark Twain had a thoughtful interest in history, and read it continually. He knew intimately the terrible conditions under which people had to live generations ago in all countries. He was always for the underdog and against pretense, and he felt

that the legend, beautiful as it was, should not hide the facts. In this book he proposed to poke fun at everything false from early English tales of romance to the ways of the practical American, who tried to put everything on a commercial basis. So the Yankee, through the magic of Mark Twain's pen, dropped back into King Arthur's court and transformed England in a manner wise, wonderful, and funny.

The Yankee stirred up trouble in England, for the English didn't like to laugh at themselves, as pictured in this book. They preferred the legendary portrait of their land in the year 635. Even in America some readers were offended, but there were others who liked it, including William Dean Howells, of *The Atlantic Monthly*. He compared it to the great Don Quixote of Cervantes. After a while interest in the tale picked up, people enjoyed its humor, and its comment on the strange ways of humanity. It was recognized as a great book, and later plays and movies were made of it. It is quoted, and laughed over, and read and reread today.

Mark made jokes about himself as an author, and he even said that he wrote only for money. Both those who knew him and his books themselves have proved this to be untrue. He worked seriously on his books, and although they are uneven in quality — for Mark Twain the author was as unpredictable in his writing as in his personality — some of them are permanent classics. No other writer has ever pictured the Western America of Mark Twain's youth so brilliantly or with such vivid sympathy. It took his literary friends a long time to learn this, for Mark was also a funny man. After a while even Mark Twain himself came to realize that, although he was never "an Eastern man of art and letters," he was a great literary figure. He stood tall in a way that was his own kind of genius. From the first, people understood that he was one of them. He became the most beloved of them all. He was called the "Lincoln of literature."

The Clemens family spent more time in Europe as the girls grew old enough to study. Both Mark and Livy enjoyed living abroad, and the time came when they were also glad to save expenses by living there. Mark was able to write in other countries as well as at home, and his increasing business worries seemed a little farther away from him when he traveled. A book for boys called *Tom Sawyer Abroad* and *The Tragedy of Pudd'nhead Wilson* were written in Europe, and it was while he lived abroad during a nine-year period there, coming back to America from time to time, that he began a long cherished book. This was *The Personal Recollections of Joan of Arc*. The first interest in the tragic story of the "Maid of Orleans" had come to him on the streets of Hannibal. The book was twelve years in preparation, and its writing covered two years.

During this time of wandering Mark happened to meet the Prince of Wales. Prince Edward said gravely, "It is a great

pleasure, Mr. Clemens, to have met you — again."

"Have we met before?" asked a surprised Mark.

"Oh, yes," replied the Prince with a smile. "Don't you remember that day in Oxford Street when I was leading a procession and you were on top of a bus in your new overcoat with flap pockets?"

No man ever enjoyed popularity more than Mark Twain, even though the shadows were closing on him again. This time his anxiety was about his financial situation. Like his stern father, his lovable and rather comic brother Orion, and his uncle James Lampton, whom he portrayed in *The Gilded Age,* Samuel Clemens was given to vast but impractical enthusiasms.

He tried out the first fountain pen, which leaked ink all over his table, the first typewriter, not yet perfected, and the early telephone. He was enthusiastic about mental telepathy, mental healing, about osteopathy, and about one of the first phonographs. He made some unprofitable inventions himself,

129

and backed others with large sums of money. His ideas were often good, but never worked out well. Sam Clemens knew the value of a typesetting machine, but he backed the wrong invention, and sank most of his money as well as that of his wife in an intricate machine that wouldn't work. And, as if writing, and backing inventions were not enough to keep him busy, he also went into the publishing business.

This came about when he saw General Grant dying of cancer, and worried about Mrs. Grant's being left penniless. Mark persuaded Grant to write his memoirs. The publication of this book was a success, and it made Mrs. Grant's future comfortable. Flushed with this triumph Mark went on to have the Pope write his memoirs, but this turned out to be a dismal failure and caused the publishing house to go under. His personal and business accounts were a complete mess. Mark left his family in Europe and came back to America time after time, but could do nothing practical about straightening out his affairs. And then luck came to his aid, for he made a friend of Henry Rogers, a wealthy financier who took over the tangle and gradually whipped matters into shape.

When he could discover how much he owed, Mark was appalled to find that his debts came to more than $150,000. There was only one quick way for him to make money, and he had not expected to employ that way again. He determined to make a new "raid" on the lecture public and travel around the globe to do it. He would pay every cent that he owed. Livy was in better health than usual and would enjoy the trip, and Clara could go with them. Susy did not feel up to going, and Jean, so strong and chubby as a small child, had developed epilepsy in her early teens. They would live with Mrs. Crane and join their parents and sister in England at the end of the

year's tour.

The journey was another triumph for Mark Twain. His announced intention to pay his debts was cheered by his public, and he was still the most successful lecturer in the world. Vast crowds came everywhere he lectured, in India, Australia, the Pacific islands. Money flooded in from the lectures, and Mark was also taking notes for a book called *Following the Equator,* written the succeeding year. Mark's notebook recorded all that he saw, all that happened, his triumphs and his failures. It included details of personal life.

During their marriage Olivia Clemens had tried earnestly to reform some of her husband's habits and had found them too firmly rooted in the past to come loose. She made a determined effort to get Mark to give up whiskey altogether, but a compromise was reached in which Livy ceased to object to his nightly drink. Mark tried to stop smoking cigars — and that didn't last long as a reform effort. Of all his faults Livy disliked most his swearing.

From time to time Mark resolved to stop swearing. One of these resolutions was made on shipboard on the Indian Ocean.

131

He was taking his tonic, bottle in one hand, medicine glass in the other, bottle cork in teeth. He had poured a glass of water and put it on the basin. The ship lurched, the glass crashed, and as he tried to throw the broken glass out of the porthole; he threw the medicine glass instead. Then, the record in his notebook read, "I released my voice." When the flow of expletives had run down he heard a quiet voice behind him, saying, "Don't reform any more, Youth. It's not an improvement."

At the end of that year, when they arrived in England, Mark knew that he had earned enough to pay his debts in full, and had some money left over. Now he could be happy again; now the girls and Katy Leary, their old nurse, could join them. It was then that a cable came from Katy saying that Susy was seriously ill. Mrs. Clemens and Clara took the next ship for America, and Mark waited anxiously. While they were still at sea another cable arrived telling of the death of Susy from meningitis. The only grain of comfort her father had was that she died in her home in Hartford, and that she had had with her her Aunt Sue, Joe Twitchell, other old friends, and Katy Leary.

Susy's mother and sister arrived in time only to stand beside her grave in Elmira, when she was buried in the family plot beside her little brother. A few weeks later Mrs. Clemens and Clara returned to England, bringing Jean and Katy Leary. The family moved into a rented house in London, where they lived quietly for some months. Mark, who could never be long away from his writing, took up his pen again. He worked steadily on his new travel book telling of the year's journey just ended.

A PREVIEW OF

A Connecticut Yankee
in KING ARTHUR'S COURT

What would it be like to wake up one morning and find oneself in the sixth century instead of the Twentieth? When that happened to a Yankee from Connecticut he was bewildered, to say the least. Yet, since he was a practical as well as a resourceful man, he set out at once to take charge of the situation. At King Arthur's court he realized that he had certain advantages over these knights and ladies. One little item was the fact that he knew what had happened to the world during the centuries after these people had died. His knowledge, which went forward as well as backward, made it possible for him to work miracles of a most impressive kind.

Like all Yankees this one was energetic and smart. He could easily produce machines that would not be invented for several centuries. He could also try to bring about some much needed changes in living conditions. Nevertheless all of his efforts collided head-on with the way of thinking of those who lived "when knighthood was in flower," and his troubles multiplied. Inventing the telephone wasn't too difficult, but how could he get out of a jousting tournament with Sir Sagramor?

The sixth century might be romantic, but it just wasn't up to date. Now and then the Yankee's cocky confidence in his ability to get things done plunged downward as he came up against a lot of opposition. Maybe those knights in their rattling armor were better fighters than he had realized. He might look with scorn on magicians and their spells, yet did he really know that his modern ideas could win against them? Maybe the sixth century possessed knowledge of real magic that had been lost since then. The Yankee was up against old Merlin the Mage, best wizard of all time, and Merlin was an enemy to be feared.

8

Stormfield

THE GRIEVING Clemens family could not live in retirement long, for the world sought out Mark Twain. They traveled about Europe, always welcomed everywhere, and Mark Twain was recognized on the streets of Paris, London, Berlin, Vienna, Rome — anywhere, it seemed, by anyone who came along. He appeared to be a friend to all, rich and poor, famous and obscure. When Mark heard of a new treatment for Jean's epileptic seizures, he took the family to Sweden to try it. After that they went from doctor to doctor, in different countries, but nothing helped. Along with this constant worry about their younger daughter they had a full-scale social life.

In London Mark attended a luncheon, and was one of the last to leave. He was surprised to find that a clergyman had taken his hat by mistake. So Mark put on the clerical head-gear of Canon Wilberforce and wore it home. Then he sat down and wrote a note to the good clergyman telling him that a strange thing had happened. Suddenly, Mark said, he had been unable to tell anything but the truth — and his morals and character had so improved that his family had grown alarmed. Then he had discovered the reason! He was wearing the canon's hat. He trembled for the clergyman, who must be wearing his. Oddly enough, Mark's note crossed one sent by the canon, in which the latter said that his usual tiresome conversation had abruptly become lively and witty, something he failed to understand until he discovered that the historic name of Mark Twain was in his hat. He asked whether Mark had suffered from dullness and had wondered why.

The Clemens family wanted to go home. Feeling, somehow, that they could not go back to Hartford without Susy, they went to New York City and rented a house near Washington Square. America rejoiced to have Mark Twain at home once more. He couldn't walk down Fifth Avenue without being recognized and hailed, and this he enjoyed. Mark never took a back street, if he could help it, and he deliberately chose the time of day when crowds were thickest. Mark Twain's hair was white now, and he had white suits made to match it. These he wore both summer and winter, and nobody could fail to notice him in white with the silver curls and mustache. In earlier years he had been a bit vain of his good looks and his dark red hair, and now this particular quirk of vanity seemed to grow in him.

That summer Mark took his family to Saranac Lake, where he could work in a leafy quiet on the shore near their cottage. He was writing articles for magazines as well as stories and letters to newspapers. He was considered an authority, and everything that he wrote was read. He expressed his strong views on the right or wrong of daily happenings, and sometimes he could not resist a joke. Since those days in Hannibal when he had stirred up trouble for Orion, he had enjoyed a hoax. His last hoax, one that gave him much pleasure, was a purely literary one.

Into a parody on the popular Sherlock Holmes stories he

inserted a paragraph full of verbal impossibilities from beginning to end. Yet it read so smoothly, and so poetically, that few readers caught the subtle absurdity of it. Only in the last line did he give it away explicitly, when he wrote solemnly that "far in the empty sky a solitary oesophagus slept upon motionless wing."

The letters that this brought him from all over the English-speaking world filled Mark with delight. But he was so snowed under with mail that he saw no way to handle the situation except to confess publicly, quoting several of the letters. He said that he meant to take in only the innocent, but that he had fetched the guilty as well. He was especially pleased that a professor in the Philippines thought the passage beautiful except for that "curious creature that slept upon motionless wing," and Mark couldn't help quoting another teacher in New England who wrote, "I'll be eternally cussed if I can make it out."

In April, 1902, Mark Twain was honored by having a degree conferred on him by the University of Missouri. He returned to his home state for this ceremony, then went back to visit the river. He saw his old friend, river pilot Horace Bixby, and found him to be still youthful and spry, although years older than Mark. There, in the Planters Hotel in St. Louis, pilots gathered to greet Mark Twain, and he had a grand time swapping yarns with them. Then he moved on to the town of his boyhood.

Hannibal turned out its own kind of "red carpet" for its famous local boy. The friends of his youth who were still alive were there, although many were missing. Mark spent five days attending everything from school commencement to Sunday School.

At the Hannibal school he handed out diplomas without bothering about correct names, telling each boy and girl to "take a good one. Don't take two, but be sure to pick a good one." In Sunday School he told stories that were not in the Sunday School books. One of the stories, he said, taught the value of perseverance. It was about a workman drilling for some blasting on Holliday's Hill, and how, when the dynamite went off too soon, the man shot up until he disappeared. Then he came down, landing upright — and kept on drilling. "Just persevering you see, and sticking to his work. Little boys and girls," said Mark Twain, "that's the secret of success, just like that poor but honest workman on Holliday's Hill." Then he finished by saying that the man was docked in his pay by his foreman for the fifteen minutes that he was up in the air.

It was after this trip that his beloved Livy became ill with a heart condition. Life in the city was too strenuous for her, and so Mark accompanied his wife and two daughters to a large rented house in Riverdale, a few miles up the Hudson River from New York City. When Livy grew gradually worse and her doctors recommended a warm climate, Mark took his family to a villa on the hills overlooking Florence, Italy. Livy was no better there. She lived until June, and then on a soft warm evening, as Mark played the piano downstairs and sang the old Negro songs that he loved so well, Livy smiled at the sound of his music. When he went up to say goodnight he was told that with the last notes of his song she had left him. Some time later Mark wrote a delicate and moving tribute to his wife. He called it *Eve's Diary* and it ends with Adam at Eve's grave, "Wheresoever she was, *there* was Eden."

Mark returned to America, with Jean, Clara, and Katy Leary, to bury Olivia Clemens in Elmira. Then he went to New York

and settled again near Washington Square. During her mother's long illness Clara had borne the brunt of running the family and of Jean's care, for Jean's health had not improved. Now Clara had to go to a rest home to recover her own health.

Mark was much alone, except for his friends. Dressed in his brilliant dressing gown, he wrote in the huge carved bed that he and Livy had bought in Venice years before. Here he received visitors, and here he began to dictate his biography to Albert Bigelow Paine, a young writer who became the loyal friend of his old age.

Paine brought in a stenographer, and Mark found talking an ideal way to put down the record of his remarkable life. In the afternoons he played billiards with Paine, and in the evenings he went out with his friends. All of his life fate had held out to him personal disaster and great grief with one hand — and in the other had offered him friendship. He took Jean to the country for the summer, and Paine came along to continue the biography.

Mark Twain could not feel at home in a household without cats, and so for this summer he rented a mother cat and her kittens from a neighbor. They provided both amusement and companionship for him indoors and out.

The following winter Clara returned to her family, her health restored and her talent for music once again her special interest. That winter Mark became a particular friend of a remarkable young girl who was without sight or hearing and whose name was Helen Keller. Many came and went in the house on lower Fifth Avenue, and the long biography made good progress.

Mark had reached the time of life when old friends pass away. He had made a sad journey back to Hartford to the funeral of Charles Dudley Warner. He went to the funeral of Patrick McAleer, his Irish coachman and friend since his marriage day. When he was asked by a reporter for a definition of a gentleman, he gave a moving tribute to Patrick McAleer, "an ideal gentleman."

Apart from the biography Mark was not doing much now, only an occasional article or magazine story. But he had a long row of books on his shelves. They were as popular as ever, and they continued to bring in a large income.

Of all his own books his favorite was *Personal Recollections of Joan of Arc*. This story he had read to Olivia and his three daughters as he wrote it in Europe, and it had been their favorite too. *Joan* was a serious book, and because Mark thought that the public would expect too much humor in it he had not signed his name. Yet no one could mistake the author of a Mark Twain book, for it had his character and his style. It is generally agreed that Mark Twain's greatest books are *Tom Sawyer, Huckleberry Finn,* and *Life on the Mississippi,* for these books are America, and Mark Twain is uniquely American. Nevertheless he loved his *Joan* best, and it is a book that is, and always will be, well worth reading for its excitement and its tenderness.

Personal Recollections of
JOAN OF ARC

For most of his lifetime Mark Twain was devoted to Joan of Arc, the shepherdess. Even while writing other books, he studied her history and the documents relating to her that were on record in France. In 1428 that nation was in its darkest hour, torn apart by war and betrayed by its leaders. Why should a simple village maid hear the voices of angels telling her to put the Dauphin on the throne of his fathers, and lead the French armies into battle? What kind of a girl was she? And how amazing it was that she could convince the prince that God had chosen her to be the savior of France! The young girl became a warrior, bearing a banner emblazoned with the lilies of France. Men came from the furthermost corners of the land to follow her standard. She was a general, winning victory after victory. And then, when she had done all that her voices had commanded her to do, she was betrayed.

Joan of Arc, delivered to her enemies by the prince whom she had made king, was thrown into a dungeon. Her trial, in which the English and the church together were her accusers, branded her a sorceress. Would any woman but a witch wear the clothing of a man? Were Joan's voices from God or were they from the devil? Was it a miracle, or was it witchcraft, that made it possible for an ignorant peasant maid to be a great military leader? The people of France and the soldiers who had followed her refused to believe that her trial was legal, or her sentence just. Yet these soldiers, who had fought bravely for France and for the Maid of Orleans, could not save her.

A crowd gathered in the market square of Rouen to watch the burning of Joan of Arc. Even the English soldiers felt compassion for her, and one of them handed her a cross made of two sticks of wood. When her ashes were cast into the River Seine, many Frenchmen called Joan a martyr, and five hundred years later the church made her a saint. Mark Twain put his own feeling into the words of one of Joan's friends—"that image, untouched by time or decay, has remained with me all my days."

9

The Comet Returns

Mark Twain never expected to cross the water again, but in 1907 he sailed once more for England to receive an honorary degree from Oxford University. No other honor of this kind could have so pleased him. When he arrived in London he received a welcome such as royalty seldom gets, and from the time that he set foot on the dock Mark was in his element, surrounded by people. England, anger at *The Yankee* forgotten, welcomed her favorite American with a joke. It happened that the Ascot Race Cup had just been stolen, and so the newspapers carried headlines reading: MARK TWAIN ARRIVES — ASCOT CUP STOLEN. Then some famous jewels disappeared, and again the newspapers joyously proclaimed the fact that Twain was in England.

Mark enjoyed the joke, and made a statement to the press denying most seriously that he had stolen the Ascot Cup. He said that he had never stolen anything in England except a hat, and that was only a clergyman's hat and not worth much. Mark also read a note from his daughter Clara, in which she gave him some social instructions, as his wife had always done. He remembered that once when he was invited to the White House by President Cleveland he had found a note in his evening clothes. Livy had written, "Don't wear your arctics in the White House," and Mark had asked Mrs. Cleveland to write on it "He didn't."

Mark called this kind of thing "dusting off Papa." Reporters had printed a story saying that the great Mark Twain had gone across the street from his hotel to a club in a sky-blue bathrobe and slippers. Reading this, Clara had sent a "dusting-off cable" which read: "Much worried. Remember proprieties." She received a cabled reply, "They all pattern after me." And he denied that he had gone out in the street in a sky-blue bathrobe anyway; it was his old brown one.

The ceremonies at Oxford were brilliant and interesting. Among those who received degrees, clad in crimson robes, were Rudyard Kipling, the sculptor Auguste Rodin, General William Booth of the Salvation Army, the Prime Minister, princes, and prelates. Yet of them all Mark Twain, of Hannibal, Missouri, U.S.A., was the most striking. Crowds pushed forward trying to catch a glimpse of his gray eyes under bushy white brows, and serious face with the mop of silver hair. Sam Clemens had come a long way from the banks of the broad river cleaving the western continent of America. Yet Mark Twain was only, and always, himself — enjoying his honors, enjoying his fame, yet looking at it all with that twinkle in his eyes.

When he was ready to return home, Mark Twain was guest of honor at a huge banquet and, so that he might return with his spoils, he was presented with a replica of the Ascot Cup.

Back in New York once more he decided to establish a final home in the country. He bought a large piece of land at Redding, Connecticut, next to the home of Albert Bigelow Paine, and there had a fine house built. He called it Stormfield, for one of his shorter books, *Extract from Captain Stormfield's Visit to Heaven* — a book that he wanted published only after he died. There, with Clara and Jean he hoped to make a real home again.

Mark had a billiard room, of course, and cats to keep him company. Guests decided that each room must have been provided with its own quota of cats, for there seemed to be so many. Jean was contented there with some beloved farm animals to care for, and Clara came and went as the engagements of her blossoming musical career dictated.

Jokes were still played on Mark Twain by his friends, as a matter of course. The whole household was thrown into an uproar of dismay when word came that an elephant was being sent to the master of the house. Things eased somewhat with

the news that it was only a baby elephant. A few days later a circus trainer arrived with several bales of hay, and a place was selected for the little pachyderm to live inside the large conservatory. Then the elephant arrived. It proved to be a toy, expertly made and large, but not lively enough to cause trouble.

Mark Twain became interested in a new library for the nearby town of Redding. He astonished his visitors by having contribution boxes set up in prominent places in his home. If a friend came to play billiards he was not allowed to leave before giving to the library.

Having no grandchildren, Mark Twain "adopted" many children as friends in his old age. He had several honorary grandsons, the children and grandchildren of his friends, but he was especially interested in his "granddaughters." The little girls reminded him of his own three girls in those happy years with Livy in Hartford and at Quarry Farm. Mark called these children his "Angel Fish Club" and gave the little girls enameled

pins made in that shape. During winters that he came to spend in Bermuda he made companions of the small girls who were there, and they all joined the "Angel Fish Club."

In the autumn of 1909, when trees flamed and burned with color, there was a wedding at Stormfield. Clara Clemens married Ossip Gabrilowitsch, a distinguished pianist whom she and her family had known for some years in Europe. Her father, wearing his crimson Oxford robe by request of the bride, gave his daughter away. Jean was her sister's bridesmaid. Then Mark and Jean settled down for a winter together at Stormfield, after Mark returned from a short visit to Bermuda. On December 24, when the ground was white with snow, Jean, who had happily decorated a tree and had wrapped gifts in bright papers for Christmas Day, did not come down to breakfast. Her old nurse, Katy, went upstairs and found that Jean had died of a sudden heart attack early that morning.

Once more Mark had been struck down by the tragic hand —

157

and once more the hand of friendship was held out to him. Clara was in Europe, and could not come because her husband was ill. But Mark's friends, old and new, gathered to help him through this new sorrow. Paine and his wife and daughters took over his house for him, and Mark, who had already suffered several mild heart attacks himself, returned to Bermuda to stay there with friends for the winter.

When April came and life in the New England hills once more blossomed into bud and leaf, Mark Twain was very ill. Paine went to Bermuda to bring him back home, not knowing whether he would reach port with Mark Twain alive or not. Yet in spite of great weakness, Mark finally looked again on Stormfield, and was glad to be home. Clara and Gabrilowitsch arrived, and Mark smiled and talked to them.

On April 20 Halley's comet appeared — sweeping across the sky with its same flaming tail. This was its first return to the sight of earthbound eyes in seventy-six years, the same comet that crossed the dark night sky so long before, when a sickly, red-haired boy had been born in Florida, Missouri, of parents named Clemens. It was Mark Twain's own comet. Once he had said, "I came with the comet. I will go with it." The day after the comet's coming he closed his eyes on the world for the last time.

Mark Twain — great wit, great democrat — was first beloved because he was a wonderfully funny man, in person and in his writings. Then he was recognized as the foremost recorder of the quality of American life of his youth. Then people began to realize that he was more than that, that he was a master of satire and something of a philosopher. In his own lifetime he was quoted everywhere, and still is today. In books and magazines and newspapers, on movie screens, on television and on radio — Mark Twain's quaint and wise remarks are read and heard, and remembered.

The early bird doesn't always get the worm — I knew a man once who got up early — and was kicked by a horse.

Everybody talks about the weather — and nobody does anything about it!

Training is everything — cauliflower is nothing but cabbage with a college education.

When angry count four — when very angry, swear!

Once he had written, "Let us endeavor so to live that when we come to die even the undertaker will be sorry."

Now it was the whole world that was sorry, and mourned his passing. His friend Howells had said of him, "He will be remembered with the great humorists of all time. None of them was his equal in humanity."

Several years before he died Mark Twain had amused himself by advertising in a newspaper for his obituary, saying that he wished to choose his own. People all over the country sent in their suggestions. There were many good ones — and one that he enjoyed especially. It was remembered as the comet streaked across the dark sky:

"Death finds a shining Mark."